WILDERNESS SURVIVAL GUIDE FOR KIDS

Camping and Outdoor Training Activities for Building Fires, Basic First Aid, Sourcing Food and Water and Beginner Survival Skills

By

CATHERINE YOUNG

BLUE PANDA BOOKS

© COPYRIGHT 2023 BY BLUE PANDA BOOKS- ALL RIGHTS RESERVED.

Without the prior written permission of the Publisher, no part of this publication may be stored in a retrieval system, replicated, or transferred in any form or medium, digital, scanning, recording, printing, mechanical, or otherwise, except as permitted under 1976 United States Copyright Act, section 107 or 108. Permission concerns should be directed to the Publisher's permission department.

LEGAL NOTICE

This book is copyright protected. It is only to be used for personal purposes. Without the author's or Publisher's permission, you cannot paraphrase, quote, copy, distribute, sell, or change any part of the information in this book.

DISCLAIMER NOTICE

This book is written and published independently. Please keep in mind that the material in this publication is solely for educational and entertaining purposes. All efforts have provided authentic, up-to-date, trustworthy, and comprehensive information. There are no express or implied assurances. The purpose of this book's material is to assist readers in having a better understanding of the subject matter. The activities, information, and exercises are provided solely for self-help information. This book is not intended to replace expert psychologists, legal, financial, or other guidance. If you require counseling, please get in touch with a qualified professional. By reading this text, the reader accepts that the author will not be held liable for any damages, indirectly or directly, experienced due to the information included herein, particularly, but not limited to, omissions, errors, or inaccuracies. You are accountable for your decisions, actions, and consequences as a reader.

A FREE GIFT TO OUR READERS!

Get FREE, unlimited access to it and all our new books by joining our community!

SCAN WITH YOUR CAMERA TO JOIN!

TABLE OF CONTENT

BEFORE YOU START!...	6
What This Book Will Be About.....................................	8
Part 1: Lost Or On An Adventure?...............................	13
The Fundamentals...	15
1.1 When You Get Separated.....................................	16
1.2 Awareness and Senses..	19
1.3 What You Feel & What You Shouldn't Feel.........	21
Part 2: Observation Skills..	24
Survival Kit A: Flora & Fauna.....................................	26
2.1 Look Out For Dangerous Plants...........................	27
2.2 Facts About Most Common Animals...................	52
2.3 Look Out For Dangers From Animals.................	64
Part 3: Inventory Skills..	79
Survival Kit B: Resourcing Food & Water.................	81
3.1 Foraging & Cooking Food.....................................	82
3.2 Food Management..	84
3.3 Water Resources & Storage.................................	86
"In The Wild Abyss"..	88

Part 4: Building Skills.. 95
Survival Kit C: Creating Your Basecamp................... 97
4.1 Gathering Important Resources............................. 98
4.2 How To Set Up Camp.. 100
4.3 Safety & Strength of Shelter................................... 103

Part 5: Vitality Skills... 105
Survival Kit D: Staying Alive/Surviving........................ 107
5.1 First Aid.. 108
5.2 Building A Fire.. 110
5.3 Tracking & Navigation... 112

Part 6: The Campy Kid.. 114
6.1 Planning... 116
6.2 How To Read Maps.. 118
6.3 Exploring The Wilderness...................................... 121
6.4 What Are You Packing?... 122
6.5 Outdoor Cooking... 125
6.6 Upward Leap.. 127
6.7 Fishful Thinking.. 131
6.8 Must Write!.. 133

Surviving The Wilderness... 135

About the Author.. 141

BEFORE YOU START!

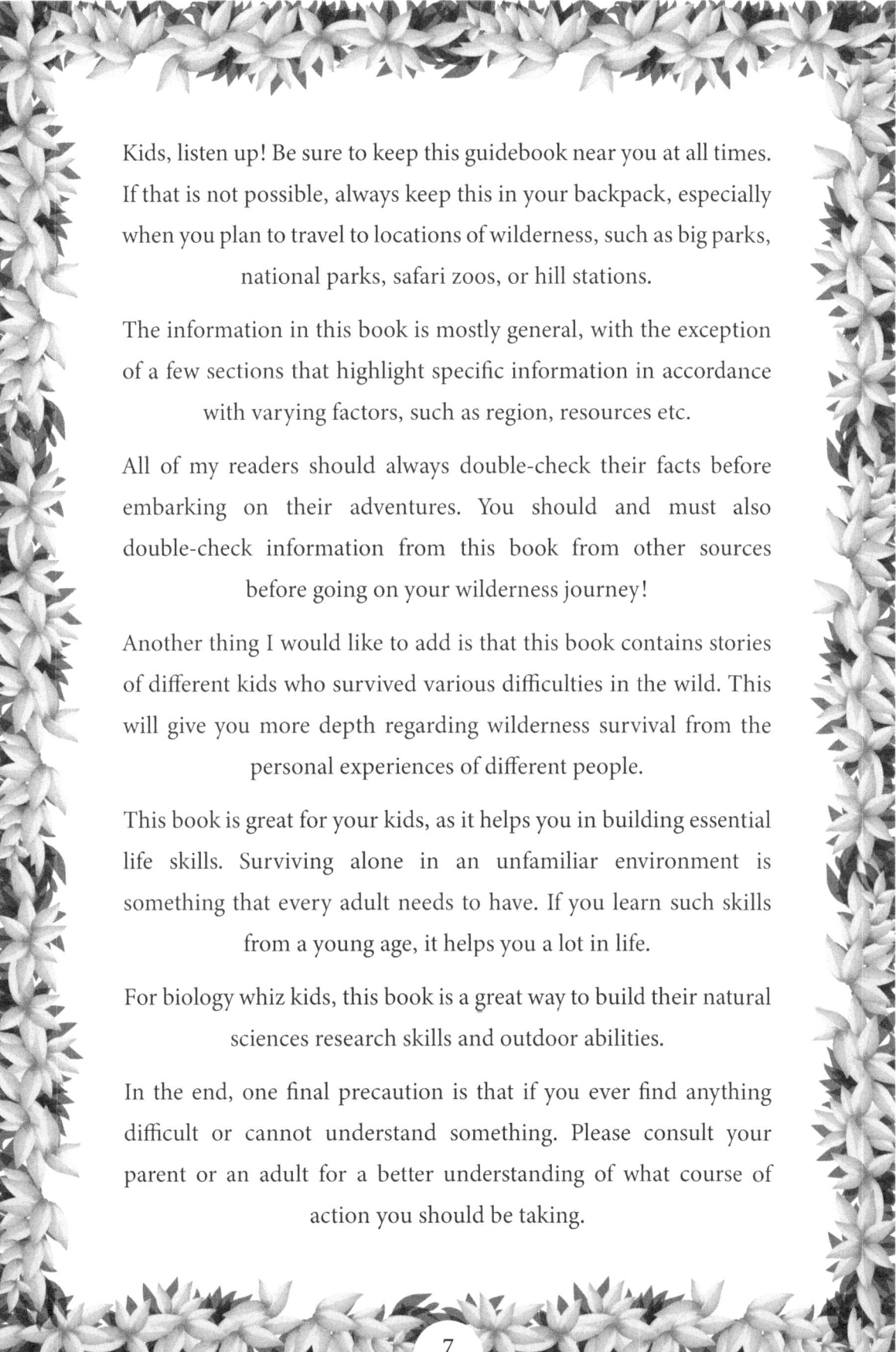

Kids, listen up! Be sure to keep this guidebook near you at all times. If that is not possible, always keep this in your backpack, especially when you plan to travel to locations of wilderness, such as big parks, national parks, safari zoos, or hill stations.

The information in this book is mostly general, with the exception of a few sections that highlight specific information in accordance with varying factors, such as region, resources etc.

All of my readers should always double-check their facts before embarking on their adventures. You should and must also double-check information from this book from other sources before going on your wilderness journey!

Another thing I would like to add is that this book contains stories of different kids who survived various difficulties in the wild. This will give you more depth regarding wilderness survival from the personal experiences of different people.

This book is great for your kids, as it helps you in building essential life skills. Surviving alone in an unfamiliar environment is something that every adult needs to have. If you learn such skills from a young age, it helps you a lot in life.

For biology whiz kids, this book is a great way to build their natural sciences research skills and outdoor abilities.

In the end, one final precaution is that if you ever find anything difficult or cannot understand something. Please consult your parent or an adult for a better understanding of what course of action you should be taking.

WHAT THIS BOOK WILL BE ABOUT

Good day to you, intrepid young travelers! Hello, and welcome to the fascinating realm of surviving in the wild! This book is going to take you on a fantastic journey filled with outdoor adventures, hands-on training, and the information you need to become a true wilderness expert. Together, we are going to begin on this journey, and it is going to be an amazing one. Are you prepared to go?

LET'S DIVE IN!

This survival handbook is designed specifically for young explorers like yourself, between the ages of 8 and 12. We are aware that you are currently in a time of life in which there are no limits to your curiosity, and the wide outdoors lures you with an infinite number of options. This book is the ideal travel companion for you, regardless of whether you've never been camping before or have a lot of experience sleeping outside.

But hold on, why do you feel the need to consult a survival guide? Isn't having fun the primary purpose of going into the wilderness? Well, of course, it's about having fun, but it's also about growing more self-reliant and building confidence in one's own talents, as well as gaining an appreciation and respect for the natural world. Imagine the sense of accomplishment you would feel if you could construct your own campfire, recognize plants that can be eaten, or had the knowledge to treat someone who has a cut or a sprain. The adventures you go on will be safer and more pleasant thanks to the abilities you've acquired.

So, what should you anticipate from reading this book? Let's take a sneak glance at some of the exciting topics that we'll be discussing in the book.

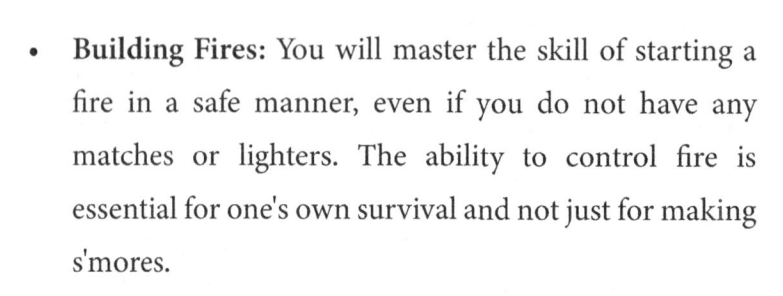

- **Building Fires:** You will master the skill of starting a fire in a safe manner, even if you do not have any matches or lighters. The ability to control fire is essential for one's own survival and not just for making s'mores.
- **Fundamental First Aid:** Although mishaps are possible, if you follow our instructions, you will be ready to treat small wounds and understand when to seek medical attention.
- **Searching For Water & Food Sources:** We will learn how and where to look for and locate water and food sources.
- **Survival Strategies:** Strategies such as building fires, gathering resources, fighting off dangerous animals, building shelter, navigation and movement in the wild will be discussed in detail. Having knowledge of these can make a huge difference when you are alone in the wilderness.

But that's not the end of it. We want you to enjoy yourself while you're reading this book so that you can retain as much information as possible. There will be fascinating challenges, quizzes, and hands-on activities for you to participate in that will put your newly acquired information to the test. In addition, we'll tell you about other young explorers who, just like you, have triumphed over the wild, and we'll supply you with advice and guidance from older people who are experienced in the outdoors.

You might be asking yourself why you should put your faith in us to be your wilderness guides at this point. However, we have you covered in that regard as well. Our group of authors and specialists has logged countless hours in the great outdoors, traversing everything from deep woods to towering mountains and expansive deserts. Along the road, we've struggled with a wide variety of obstacles, made some blunders, and picked up some important life lessons. Because we've gone where you want to go, we're able to provide you the benefit of our experience and insight.

But keep in mind that traffic might go in both directions on this roadway. Your perspective and the lessons you've learned are of equal significance.

PART 1
LOST OR ON AN ADVENTURE?

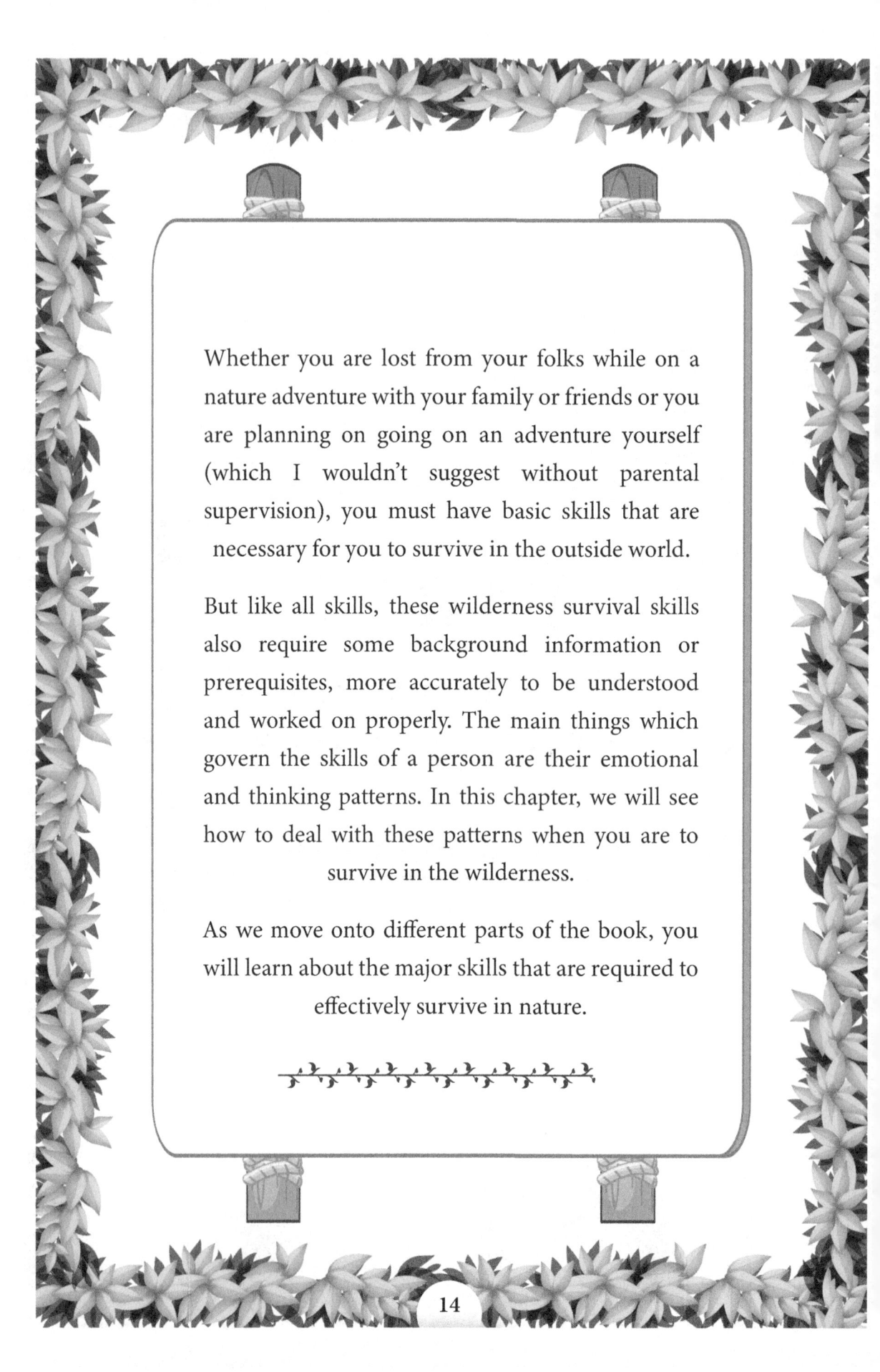

Whether you are lost from your folks while on a nature adventure with your family or friends or you are planning on going on an adventure yourself (which I wouldn't suggest without parental supervision), you must have basic skills that are necessary for you to survive in the outside world.

But like all skills, these wilderness survival skills also require some background information or prerequisites, more accurately to be understood and worked on properly. The main things which govern the skills of a person are their emotional and thinking patterns. In this chapter, we will see how to deal with these patterns when you are to survive in the wilderness.

As we move onto different parts of the book, you will learn about the major skills that are required to effectively survive in nature.

THE FUNDAMENTALS

For this first section, we will be talking about the very basics of what your emotional and mental patterns should and should not be and how they should and should not affect your survival against the wilderness.

1.1. WHEN YOU GET SEPARATED

In the event that you become separated from your family or group while you are out in the wilderness, it can be a terrifying experience; but if you are prepared with the appropriate information and mindset, you can improve your odds of securely rejoining with them. When you find yourself in this predicament, there are certain very critical things that you need to take:

- **Don't Panic!**
  First, and most importantly, you need to compose yourself and have a level head. If you panic, your judgment will get clouded, and it will be more difficult for you to make decisions that are sensible.

- **Put a Halt to It and Hear**
  Halt your movement and pay close attention to any sounds that might lead you back to the rest of your company. It's possible that they're using a whistle or calling out your name.

- **Make Use Of A Whistle**
  If you have a whistle, you can send a distress signal by blowing it in a pattern consisting of three brief bursts. This pattern is recognized. If your group is nearby, they should be able to find you with the help of this.

- **Keep Your Position**
  It is often in your best interest to remain where you are unless you are one hundred percent certain of the path back to your group. If you go further away from them, it will be more difficult for them to locate you.

- **Make Sure That People Can See You**
  Increase your visibility by waving brightly colored clothing or a reflecting object in the air if you have either of these things available to you. It is essential to the success of a reunion that you are noticed.

- **Make A Haven For Yourself**
  If you believe that you will be alone for an extended amount of time or if you are in a region that is prone to experiencing inclement weather, you should give some thought to constructing a basic shelter in order to protect yourself from the elements.

- **Keep Yourself Hydrated**
  If you have a supply of water, you should drink from it. sustaining your energy levels and sustaining mental clarity both require that you stay hydrated.

- **The Warning Flares**
  You are able to make a signal fire if you have the necessary abilities and resources. Create a smokey signal that can be seen from a considerable distance by building a fire and adding wet grass or green leaves to the flames.

1.2. AWARENESS AND SENSES

Consider implementing the following five steps to enhance your awareness and be mindful of your surroundings. It is very important to stay alert in the outdoors and this can only be achieved if you have optimized your sensory abilities.

- **Taking A Look**

  Take a moment to direct your attention towards your surroundings. Please make a mental note of any unusual sounds, unexpected movements, or objects that appear out of place in their current surroundings. Paying attention to the specifics is crucial.

- **Attend Closely and Listen**

  Pay attention for any noises of animals, water, or voices in the distance. Your ears are able to hear many sounds that your eyes could miss entirely.

- **Put Your Nose to Work**

  It is possible for your sense of smell to tip you off to the whereabouts of food, water, or even potential danger. When you're out in the outdoors, you should pay close attention to the various smells.

- **Sensitize Yourself to the Ambience**

  It is helpful to get information about the temperature and texture of items and surfaces by touching them. You can use this information to help you make more educated decisions.

- **Try It Out**

  When it comes to this sense, exercise extreme caution because tasting unidentified plants or substances can be quite hazardous. However, if you are positive about the safety of something, the information provided by your taste receptors might be really helpful.

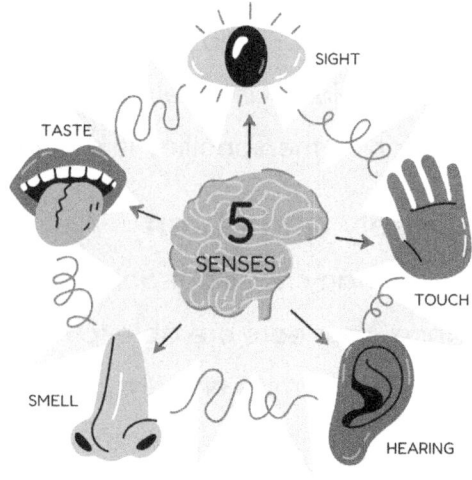

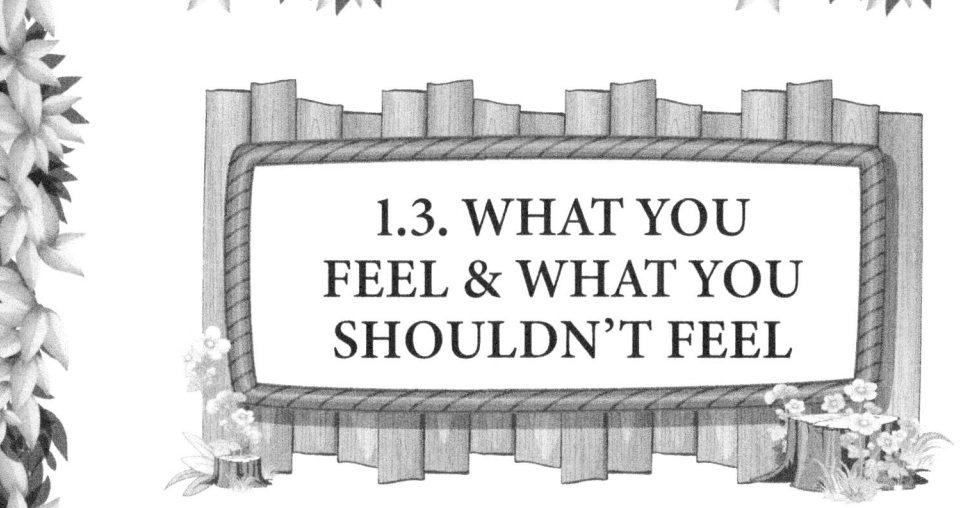

1.3. WHAT YOU FEEL & WHAT YOU SHOULDN'T FEEL

It can be helpful to your health and safety in the wilderness to be aware of what you should and should not feel when you are out there:

Feelings That Are Typical

- Feeling parched is a natural reaction, particularly when you are in a hot & dry climate. Make an effort to save water and use it in a responsible manner.
- The sensation of hunger is your body's way of communicating with you that it requires nourishment. Consume your available food supply with caution.

- Walking and trying to survive in the outdoors can be physically taxing activities that might lead to fatigue. To prevent tiredness, sleep when it's necessary.
- Fear: It's natural to experience fear when you're in an unknown environment. Make use of your fear as a driving force to keep you awake and ensure that you take the necessary precautions.

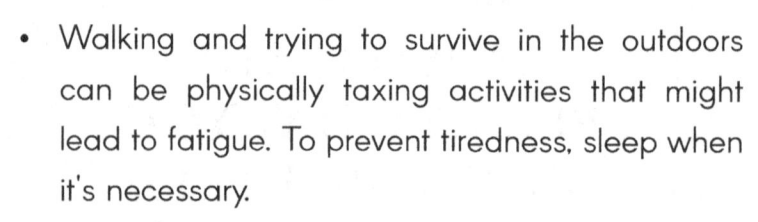

Feelings That Are Not Typical

- Although it's normal to feel worried in certain circumstances, yielding to fear is not the best course of action. Instead of submitting to your fears, focus on finding solutions to the problems you face.
- Extreme Pain: Severe pain, on the other hand, may point to a sickness or injury that demands quick medical attention. Do not ignore it; if possible, seek first aid or medical assistance.
- Tingling or numbness are two symptoms that may indicate an injury or prolonged exposure to extremely low temperatures. Take timely action to address these concerns in order to avert further damage.

- Disorientation or Dizziness: If you suddenly feel dizzy or disoriented, it could be due to a number of different conditions, including dehydration or exhaustion. Take a short rest, drink some water, and evaluate the situation before continuing.

You will be more equipped to negotiate the challenges that the environment presents and to stay safe while you are engaged in outdoor activities if you learn to trust your instincts and have an understanding of these experiences. Keep in mind that being well-prepared and having plenty of relevant knowledge are absolutely necessary for thriving in the wild.

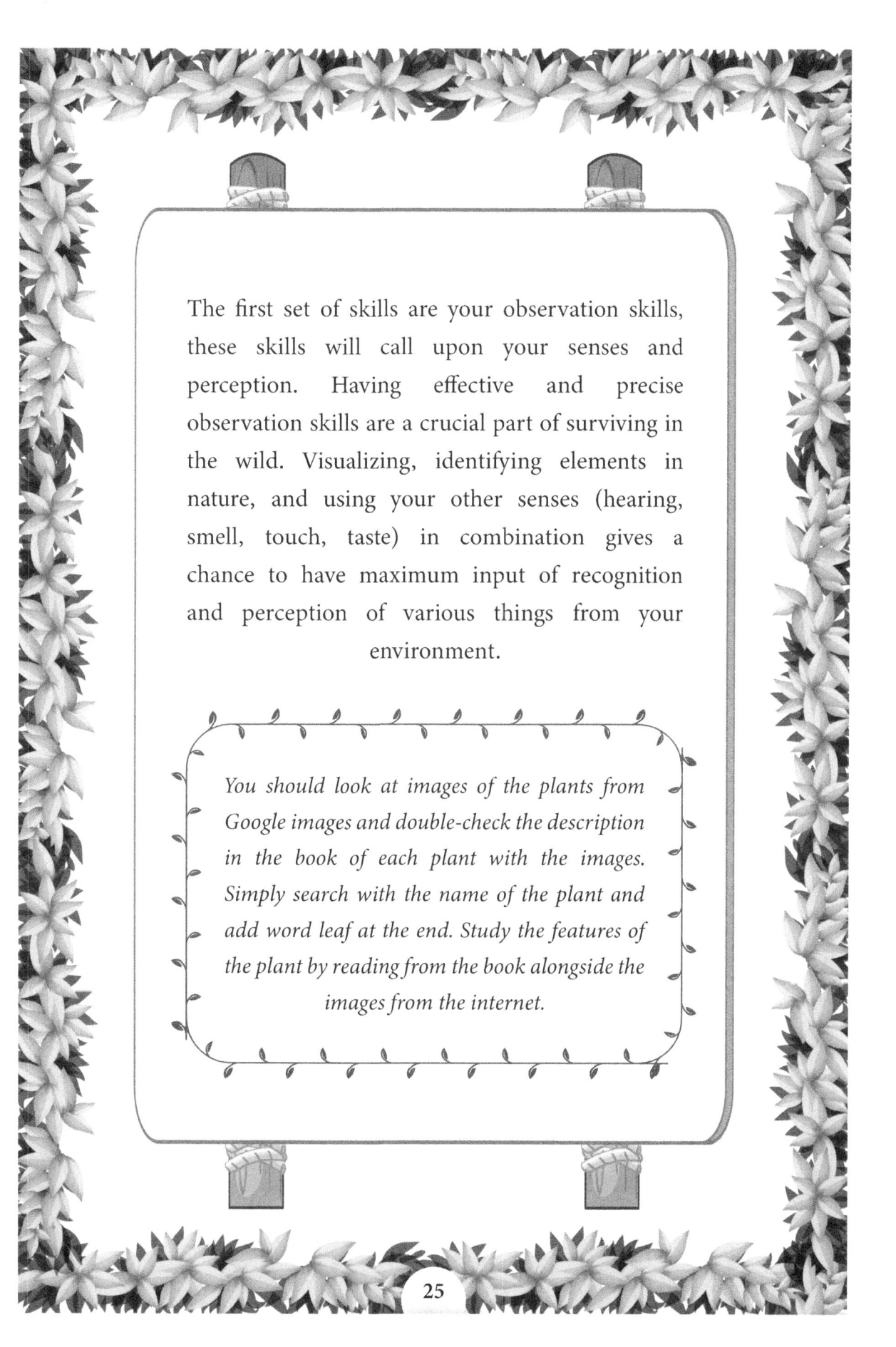

The first set of skills are your observation skills, these skills will call upon your senses and perception. Having effective and precise observation skills are a crucial part of surviving in the wild. Visualizing, identifying elements in nature, and using your other senses (hearing, smell, touch, taste) in combination gives a chance to have maximum input of recognition and perception of various things from your environment.

You should look at images of the plants from Google images and double-check the description in the book of each plant with the images. Simply search with the name of the plant and add word leaf at the end. Study the features of the plant by reading from the book alongside the images from the internet.

SURVIVAL KIT A FLORA & FAUNA

In the first chapter, we will discuss species of animals and plants in nature that are harmful or dangerous for us. It is to be noted that the species we will be talking about in this chapter are chiefly from The United States of America or Canada

The first thing that comes into the mind when anyone thinks about nature areas is the animals that inhabit them. Some animals are good, some are dangerous and we will talk about how to be safe from the dangerous ones.

2.1. LOOK OUT FOR DANGEROUS PLANTS

It is important to keep in mind that when you are out in nature, it is best to observe plants from a distance, particularly if you are unsure of what species they are. In the wild, one's safety must always come first; nevertheless, one should not let this stop them from exploring and gaining knowledge.

Poison Oak

- ### Where You'll Find It
    Poison oak is a savvy plant that grows in many parts of the United States, particularly in the western and southern parts of the country. It mostly grows in wooded areas, along paths used for hiking. It is also capable of developing into a climbing vine that can wrap itself around trees and other plants.

- How To Spot It

  The process of recognizing poison oak can be challenging at first, but as you gain experience, you'll get better at it. Here are some things that you should be on the lookout for:

  - The leaves of poison oak typically appear in clusters of three.
  - Imagine a little grouping of three leaves, and you'll have no trouble keeping this guideline in mind.
  - Leaves with rounded corners and undulating margins on all sides. Shiny and green, or tinged with a reddish color, they can also be.
  - The stems and vines of poison oak can occasionally be red, which can be used as an identifying feature for the plant.
  - Poison oak may produce white berries in the late summer or early fall. These berries are often rather tiny and white. Also, steer clear of them!

- Why and How Is It Dangerous

  Now, let's get to the meat of the matter, which is the peril posed by poison oak:

  - Poison oak, when touched, can secrete an oil called urushiol, which, when comes into contact with human skin, can cause a rash that is red and irritating, which can cause discomfort for almost two weeks.

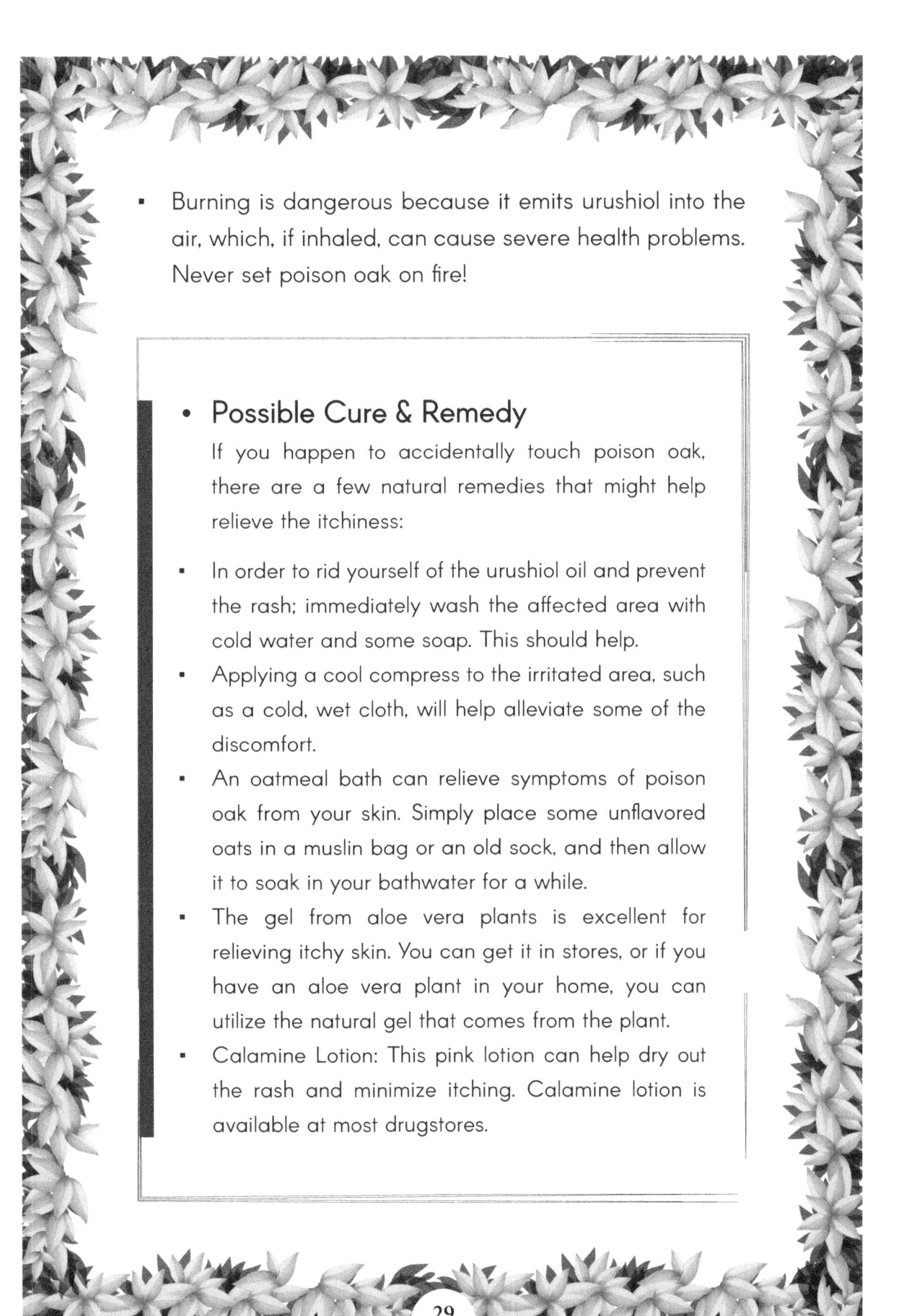

- Burning is dangerous because it emits urushiol into the air, which, if inhaled, can cause severe health problems. Never set poison oak on fire!

• Possible Cure & Remedy

If you happen to accidentally touch poison oak, there are a few natural remedies that might help relieve the itchiness:

- In order to rid yourself of the urushiol oil and prevent the rash; immediately wash the affected area with cold water and some soap. This should help.
- Applying a cool compress to the irritated area, such as a cold, wet cloth, will help alleviate some of the discomfort.
- An oatmeal bath can relieve symptoms of poison oak from your skin. Simply place some unflavored oats in a muslin bag or an old sock, and then allow it to soak in your bathwater for a while.
- The gel from aloe vera plants is excellent for relieving itchy skin. You can get it in stores, or if you have an aloe vera plant in your home, you can utilize the natural gel that comes from the plant.
- Calamine Lotion: This pink lotion can help dry out the rash and minimize itching. Calamine lotion is available at most drugstores.

Poison Ivy

- ## Where You'll Find It
  Poison ivy is a sneaky plant that may be found almost anywhere in the United States. This includes parks, and forests. It can take the form of either a low shrub or a climbing vine, and it prefers to thrive in covert locations.

- **How To Spot It**
  Poison ivy might be difficult to spot, but there are a few obvious symptoms to look out for:

  - Just like poison oak, poison ivy has clusters of three leaves. Pay close attention to this "leafy trio."
  - Almond-shaped leaves with a glossy surface are typical. They change color from green to crimson throughout the seasons.
  - The poison ivy leaf's edge may feature a few teeth or notches, much like a saw's.
  - It is a creeping shrub that hugs the ground and a climbing vine that clings to trees.

- **Why and How Is It Dangerous**
  It has the same poisonous reaction as Poison Oak!

- **Possible Natural Cure & Remedy**
  Remedies are same as Poison Oak!

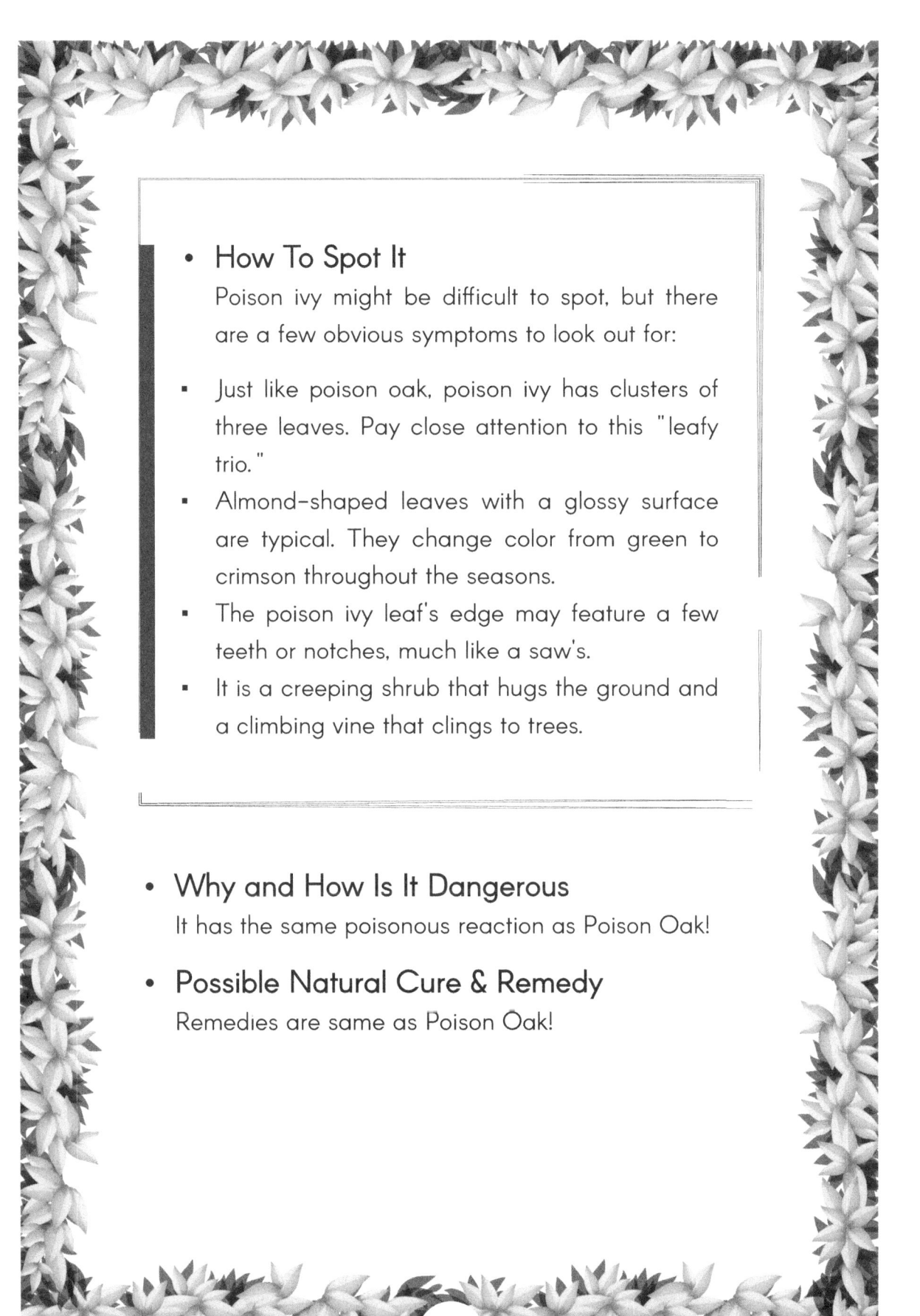

Poison Sumac

- ### Where You'll Find It

   When compared to the other plants we've looked at, hemlock stands out as unique. Hemlock is not typically found in wooded or moist environments but rather in more open settings, including fields, roadside ditches, and meadows. The tall plant's terminal clusters of tiny white blossoms stand out against the background. You should keep a safe distance from the hemlock plant at all times. Due to the fact that it is extremely dangerous and has the potential to cause death, it is not something that should be investigated or experimented with.

- **How To Spot It**

  In spite of the fact that identifying hemlock can be difficult, here are several traits that can help you spot it:

  - Hemlock is a stately tree that may reach heights of up to 10 feet, with a tall, slender trunk, and numerous branches all along its length.
  - There is a possibility that the stem will have some purplish streaks or splotches.
  - At the very tip of the stem are clusters of very tiny white flowers that are arranged in a rosette-like pattern.
  - The leaves are very finely divided, nearly exactly like the leaves of ferns, and they give the plant an air of delicacy.

- **Why and How Is It Dangerous**

  Hemlock is not like the plants that cause itching that we discussed earlier; rather, it poses a distinct kind of risk:

  - Hemlock is extremely poisonous and should be avoided. There is a lethal poison in the plant that is called "Coniine", and it may be found in all sections of the plant, including the leaves, stems, and roots.

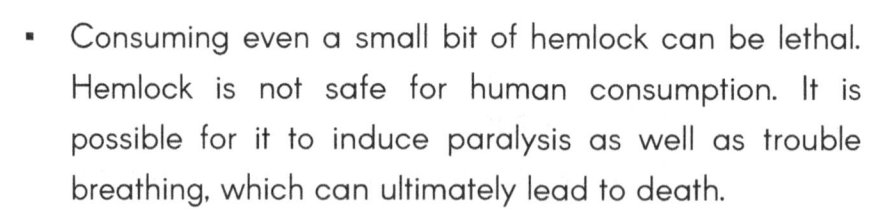

- Consuming even a small bit of hemlock can be lethal. Hemlock is not safe for human consumption. It is possible for it to induce paralysis as well as trouble breathing, which can ultimately lead to death.
- Poisoning from hemlock does not have a treatment or cure that is derived from nature. In the event that someone consumes hemlock, they should seek medical treatment as soon as possible.

- **Possible Natural Cure & Remedy**
  No home remedy exists for hemlock toxicity. Remember that this plant is toxic and should never be used for food, medication, or anything else.
  Instead, treat hemlock ingestion as follows:

- Get medical help now by calling 911 or your local emergency number.
- Keep the person calm and still while waiting for aid.
- In contrast to other plant poisonings, hemlock poisoning should not be treated by inducing vomiting. This can worsen problems.
- It's crucial to trust experienced medical specialists to provide immediate treatment.

Deadly Nightshade

- ## Where You'll Find It

    The Poisonous Nightshade is a plant that can be discovered in many places of the world, including Europe and North America. It is most common to see it growing in moist, shady settings like forests, along the banks of streams, and even in gardens. This plant thrives in cooler, shadier environments.

- **How To Spot It**

  The identification of deadly nightshade might be challenging at times, but there are a few signs that can point you in the right direction:

- It has deep purplish blooms that are bell-shaped. They dangle in a downward direction like miniature purple lanterns.
- After the blooming of the flowers, the plant will develop glossy black berries that are about the size of a marble.
- The leaves have a form similar to an oval and are often a dark green color. They are often rather huge and have undulating margins.
- Deadly Nightshade plant often takes the form of a bushy plant and can reach heights of up to three feet.

- **Why and How Is It Dangerous**

- All components of the Deadly Nightshade plant, including the leaves, stems, and flowers, are extremely poisonous. Ingestion of the leaves, berries, or even the stems of the plant can result in death due to the powerful toxins they carry.

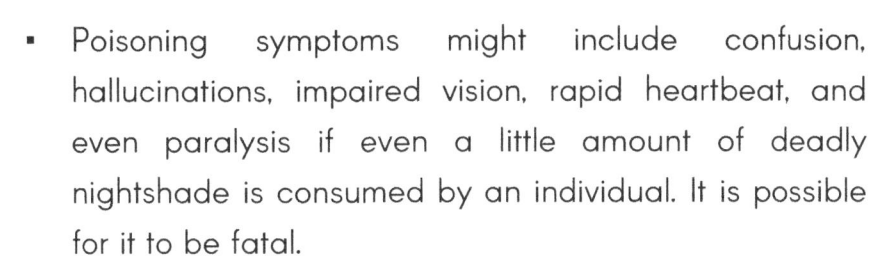

- Poisoning symptoms might include confusion, hallucinations, impaired vision, rapid heartbeat, and even paralysis if even a little amount of deadly nightshade is consumed by an individual. It is possible for it to be fatal.
- There is currently no natural treatment or cure that is known to exist for those who have been poisoned by deadly nightshade. If it is taken internally, emergency medical assistance is required for the individual.

- **Possible Natural Cure & Remedy**
  There is no natural antidote or treatment that can be administered at home for poisoning caused by Deadly Nightshade plants. Because of the extreme toxicity of this plant, quick medical attention is required. If you have reason to believe that someone has consumed deadly nightshade, you should follow the same steps as given in Hemlock.

Snowberry

- ## Where You'll Find It
  Plants of the Snowberry species are endemic to much of the US, especially the northern regions and Canada. Commonly inhabiting forests, woodlands. They are found even in gardens, grown for their ornamental value. Areas with a good amount of sunlight is best for their growth.

- ## How To Spot It
  The salient features of Snowberry are:

  - Clusters of round, small, white berries, which are one of its notable feature. They somewhat resemble snowballs, but smaller in size.
  - The leaves are not typically divided into multiple leaflets. Mostly, their margins are smooth and they have heart-like or oval shape.
  - Attaining a height of between 2 and 4 feet. They are mostly slow-growing shrubs that have many branches and stems.

- **Why and How Is It Dangerous**
   This plant may not seem dangerous, you still need to exercise caution for the following reasons:

- The snowberry plant produces white berries that, if eaten, can be fatal. If consumed, they will produce nausea, gastrointestinal distress, and other unwelcome symptoms due to the substances they contain.
- The snowberry is sometimes confused with edible berries such as blueberries and currants, which can result in accidental eating.
- Even while snowberry berries are not as harmful as the berries of certain other toxic plants, it is still advised to avoid eating them even though they are not life-threatening.

- **Possible Natural Cure & Remedy**
   There are a few things you can do in the event that someone mistakenly consumes a Snowberry or any other component of the plant and gets discomfort as a result:

- If you have reason to believe that someone has consumed snowberry, have them rinse out their mouth with a lot of water to remove any trace of the plant that may still be present.

Giant Hogweed

- ## Where You'll Find It
  Giant hogweed is a non-native, tall, and invasive plant that has established itself in various parts of North America, especially the northeastern United States and parts of Canada. Moist areas near water, such as riverbanks, ditches, and even gardens, are ideal for its growth.

- ## How To Spot It
  Despite its difficulty, Giant Hogweed can be recognized by these distinguishing characteristics:

  - This plant lives up to its monstrous reputation in terms of size. It has the potential to reach heights of 15 feet, giving it an impressive sight.
  - Giant Hogweed's leaves are up to 5 feet across, making it one of the largest plants in the world. They're deeply lobed and rough in texture, like an umbrella.
  - Stout and spotted with purple, the stems of Giant Hogweed are robust and hollow. Perhaps even their hair will be spiked.

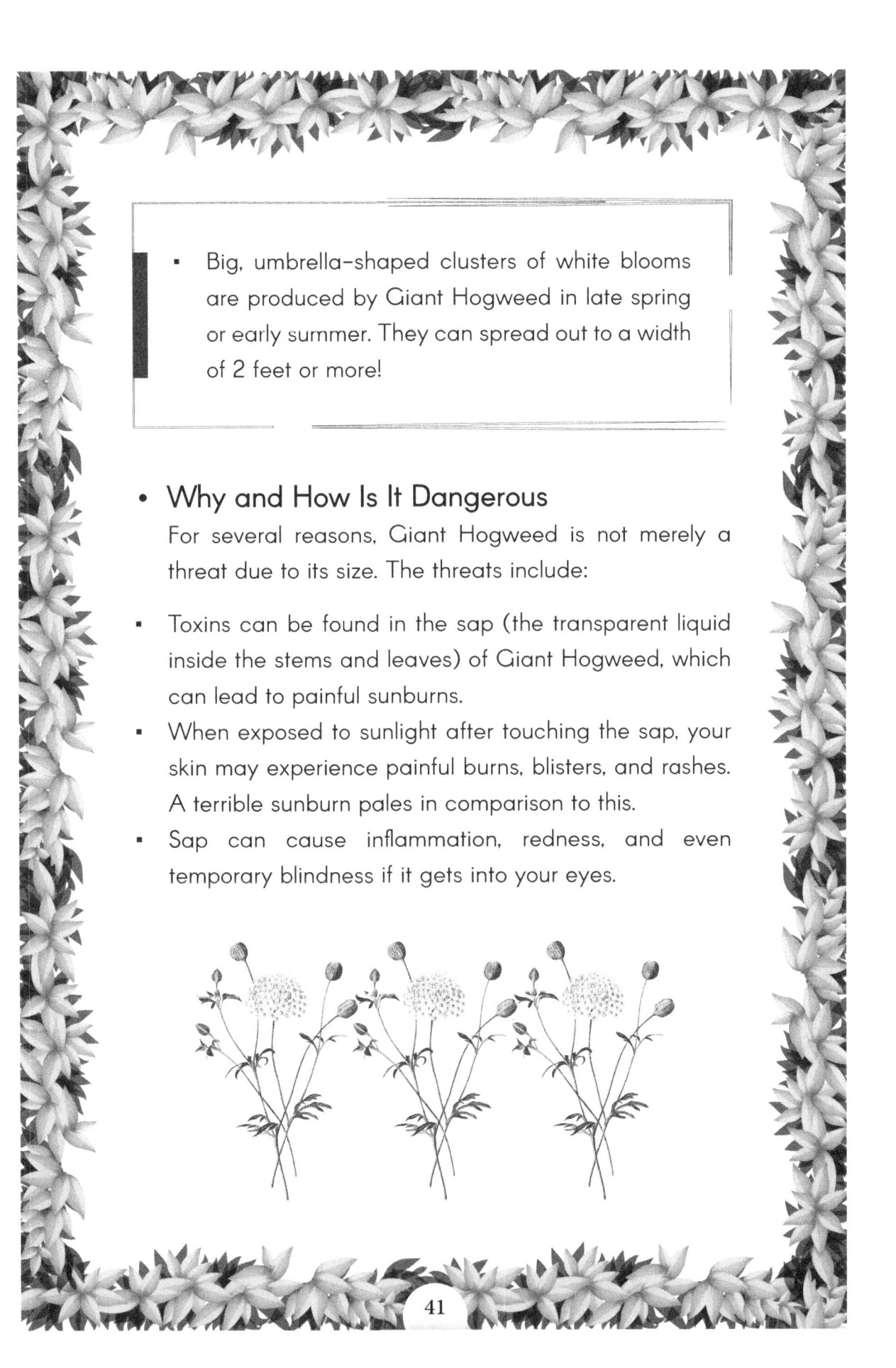

- Big, umbrella-shaped clusters of white blooms are produced by Giant Hogweed in late spring or early summer. They can spread out to a width of 2 feet or more!

Why and How Is It Dangerous

For several reasons, Giant Hogweed is not merely a threat due to its size. The threats include:

- Toxins can be found in the sap (the transparent liquid inside the stems and leaves) of Giant Hogweed, which can lead to painful sunburns.
- When exposed to sunlight after touching the sap, your skin may experience painful burns, blisters, and rashes. A terrible sunburn pales in comparison to this.
- Sap can cause inflammation, redness, and even temporary blindness if it gets into your eyes.

- **Possible Natural Cure & Remedy**

  Natural treatments for the skin response induced by Giant Hogweed are ineffective. Taking the following measures and seeing a doctor are mandatory for effective therapy.

  Here's what you can do if you come into contact with Giant Hogweed and experience skin irritation:

  - Scrub the damaged skin with cold water right away. The skin reaction can be made worse by using hot water.
  - Keep the affected region out of the sun by keeping it covered. Sunlight might exacerbate the skin reaction, thus avoiding it is essential.
  - If the skin reaction is severe or if the sap gets into your eyes, seek medical treatment right away.

Pokeweed

- ## Where You'll Find It
  Pokeweed, a genus of plants endemic to North America, grows naturally across the continent. It's a common sight in the wild, gardens, and along roadsides.

- ## How To Spot It
  Once you know what to look for, spotting Pokeweed is a breeze.

  - The bright green leaves of pokeweed are found anywhere ranging from 6-12 inches in length. They feature a simple morphology (they are not separated into leaflets) and an unusual oval shape with rounded corners.
  - Pokeweed's broad stem is typically pink or reddish-purple with green patches or streaks, but it can also be entirely green.
  - One of the most defining characteristics of pokeweed is the clusters of dark purple berries that dangle from the stem like grapes. They're alluring to the eye, but could be harmful in the long run.

- ## Why and How Is It Dangerous

  Why proper care must be taken when dealing with pokeweed:

  - Pokeweed berries and other edible parts are poisonous despite their attractive appearance. Both the plant's stem and its leaves are alive.
  - Consumption of Pokeweed berries or any other component of the plant can cause gastrointestinal distress including cramping, nausea, vomiting, and diarrhea.
  - Pokeweed has a toxic resin that is sticky and pinkish-red in color; it can cause skin and eye irritation.

- **Possible Natural Cure & Remedy**

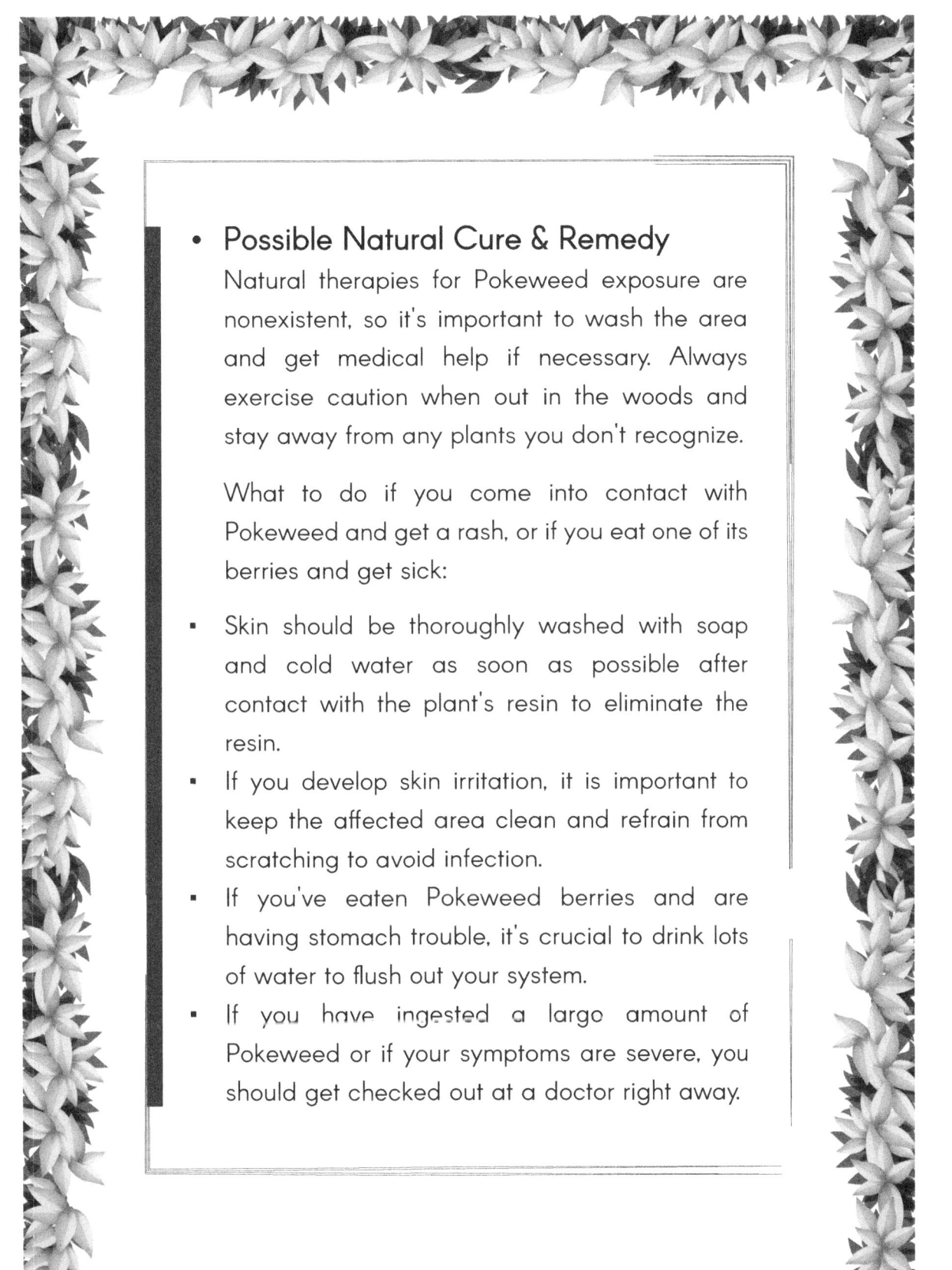

  Natural therapies for Pokeweed exposure are nonexistent, so it's important to wash the area and get medical help if necessary. Always exercise caution when out in the woods and stay away from any plants you don't recognize.

  What to do if you come into contact with Pokeweed and get a rash, or if you eat one of its berries and get sick:

- Skin should be thoroughly washed with soap and cold water as soon as possible after contact with the plant's resin to eliminate the resin.
- If you develop skin irritation, it is important to keep the affected area clean and refrain from scratching to avoid infection.
- If you've eaten Pokeweed berries and are having stomach trouble, it's crucial to drink lots of water to flush out your system.
- If you have ingested a large amount of Pokeweed or if your symptoms are severe, you should get checked out at a doctor right away.

Bittersweet

- ## Where You'll Find It

  One of the types of vines that grows in North America, particularly in the eastern parts of the United States, is called bittersweet. It can frequently be seen growing in wooded areas, along forest margins. Because of the ability of its vines to climb fences and wind around trees, it draws a lot of attention.

- ## How To Spot It

  Once you are aware of what to look for, identifying Bittersweet may be accomplished in a pretty short amount of time.

- Twisting Vines: One of the most distinguishing characteristics of bittersweet is the plant's ability to grow twisting vines that can reach a length of up to 60 feet. The vines are woody and can have a considerable amount of thickness.
- The leaves of the bittersweet plant are simple and oval in shape, with rounded corners. Typically, the leaves have a dark green color and are arranged alternately along the vine.

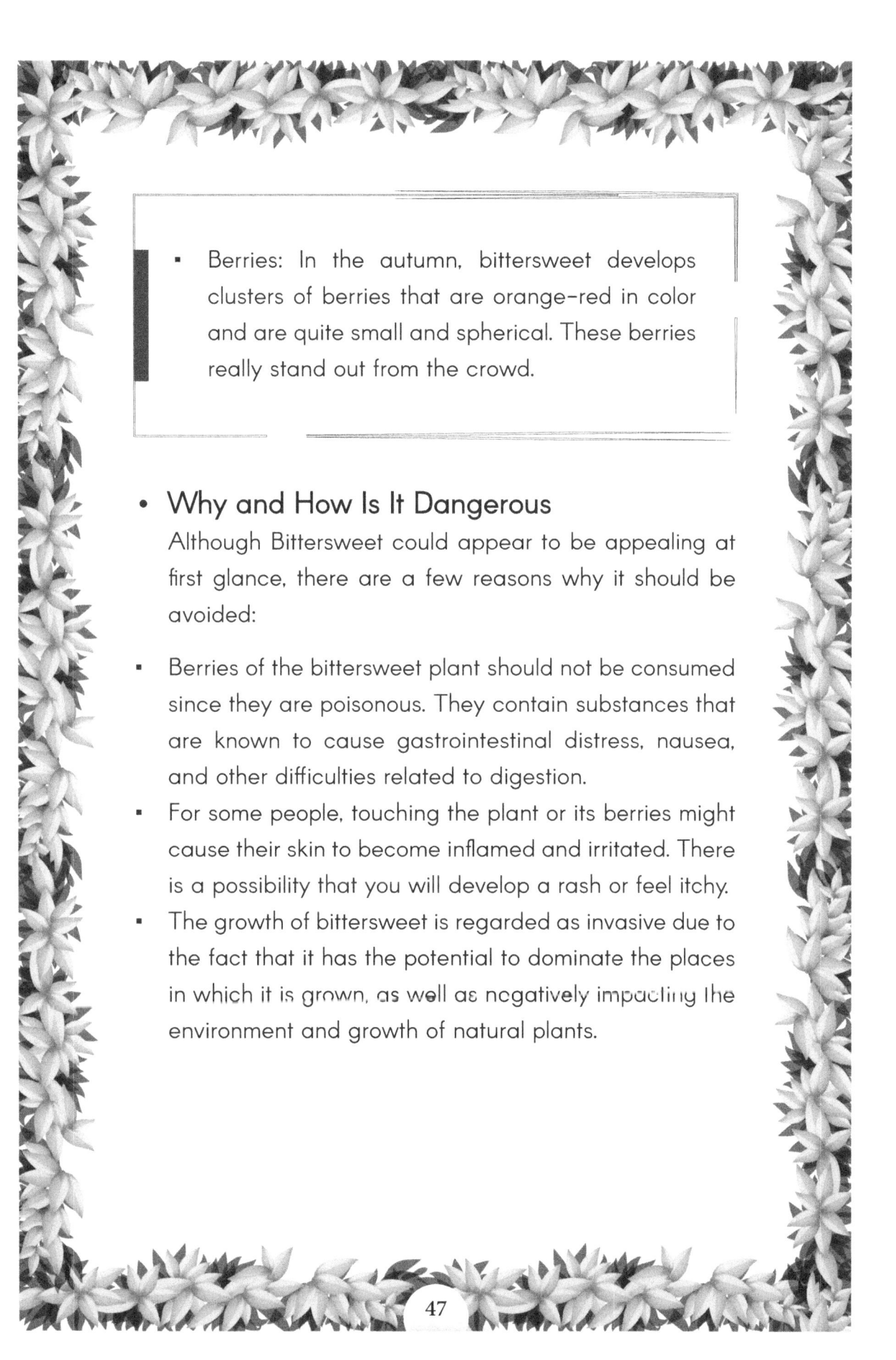

- Berries: In the autumn, bittersweet develops clusters of berries that are orange-red in color and are quite small and spherical. These berries really stand out from the crowd.

- ## Why and How Is It Dangerous
  Although Bittersweet could appear to be appealing at first glance, there are a few reasons why it should be avoided:

- Berries of the bittersweet plant should not be consumed since they are poisonous. They contain substances that are known to cause gastrointestinal distress, nausea, and other difficulties related to digestion.
- For some people, touching the plant or its berries might cause their skin to become inflamed and irritated. There is a possibility that you will develop a rash or feel itchy.
- The growth of bittersweet is regarded as invasive due to the fact that it has the potential to dominate the places in which it is grown, as well as negatively impacting the environment and growth of natural plants.

- **Possible Natural Cure & Remedy**
- There aren't any specific natural therapies for exposure to bittersweet.
- The remedy method is similar to that of Pokeweed.
- The most important thing is to clean the region that's been damaged and get medical help if you need it.
- Keep in mind that it is always preferable to err on the side of caution and refrain from handling or eating any strange plants that you find in the wild.

Stinging Nettle

- **Where You'll Find It**

   The plant known as "Stinging Nettle" can be found growing wild in a variety of regions across the globe, including North America, Europe, Asia, and Africa. It is most successful in areas with moist soil, such as forests, meadows, and areas next to streams.

- **How To Spot It**

   Once you are aware of what to look for, identifying stinging nettle is a very simple process:

   - The average height of a Stinging Nettle plant is between 2-4 ft. It differs from other types of plants in a way that it has a square stem rather than a round one.
   - These leaves are green and have a toothed or serrated edge, much to the way the edge of a saw is toothed. Leaves typically acquire heart shape and grow in a manner that mirrors one another along the stem.

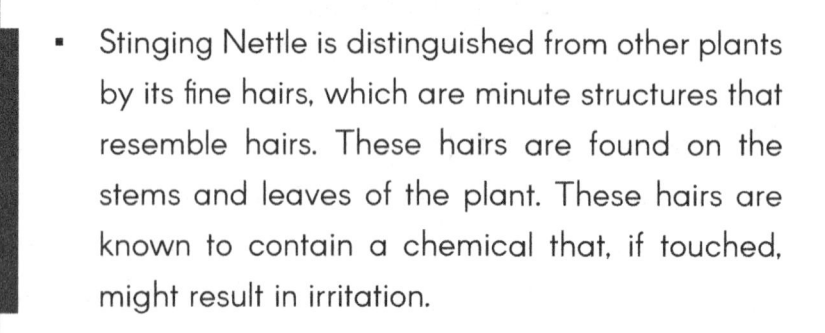

- Stinging Nettle is distinguished from other plants by its fine hairs, which are minute structures that resemble hairs. These hairs are found on the stems and leaves of the plant. These hairs are known to contain a chemical that, if touched, might result in irritation.

- ## Why and How Is It Dangerous

    Keep in mind that the discomfort caused by Stinging Nettle is just transitory and not particularly severe. It is less of a threat to one's life than it is an irritation. Throughout various civilizations, the plant has been utilized for centuries in traditional medicine, serving as a valuable resource for healing. Additionally, these cultures have also relied on the plant as a source of nourishment, incorporating it into their diets.

    While not lethal, dealing with the Stinging Nettle can be sort of a challenge due to:

    - Venomous leaves and stems that are covered with fine hairs, as previously mentioned. A rash that is mildly painful and itchy is likely to develop when your skin comes in contact with the hairs.
    - A temporary irritation that is not fatal, but can be painful. This irritation can persist for some amount of time.

- **Possible Natural Cure & Remedy**
  In the event that you touch stinging nettle by accident and end up with skin irritation, the following are some things you can do to get relief:

- To get rid of any leftover nettle hairs, you should wash the affected region as quickly as possible with lukewarm water and a gentle soap.
- Applying a cool compress to the itchy area, such as a cloth that has been soaked in cool water, can provide some comfort.
- The use of aloe vera gel on skin that has been inflamed can be beneficial. You might get some relief from the discomfort by applying it to the affected area.
- If the itching does not go away, you can try using hydrocortisone or other available over-the-counter creams to alleviate the discomfort.

2.2. FACTS ABOUT MOST COMMON ANIMALS

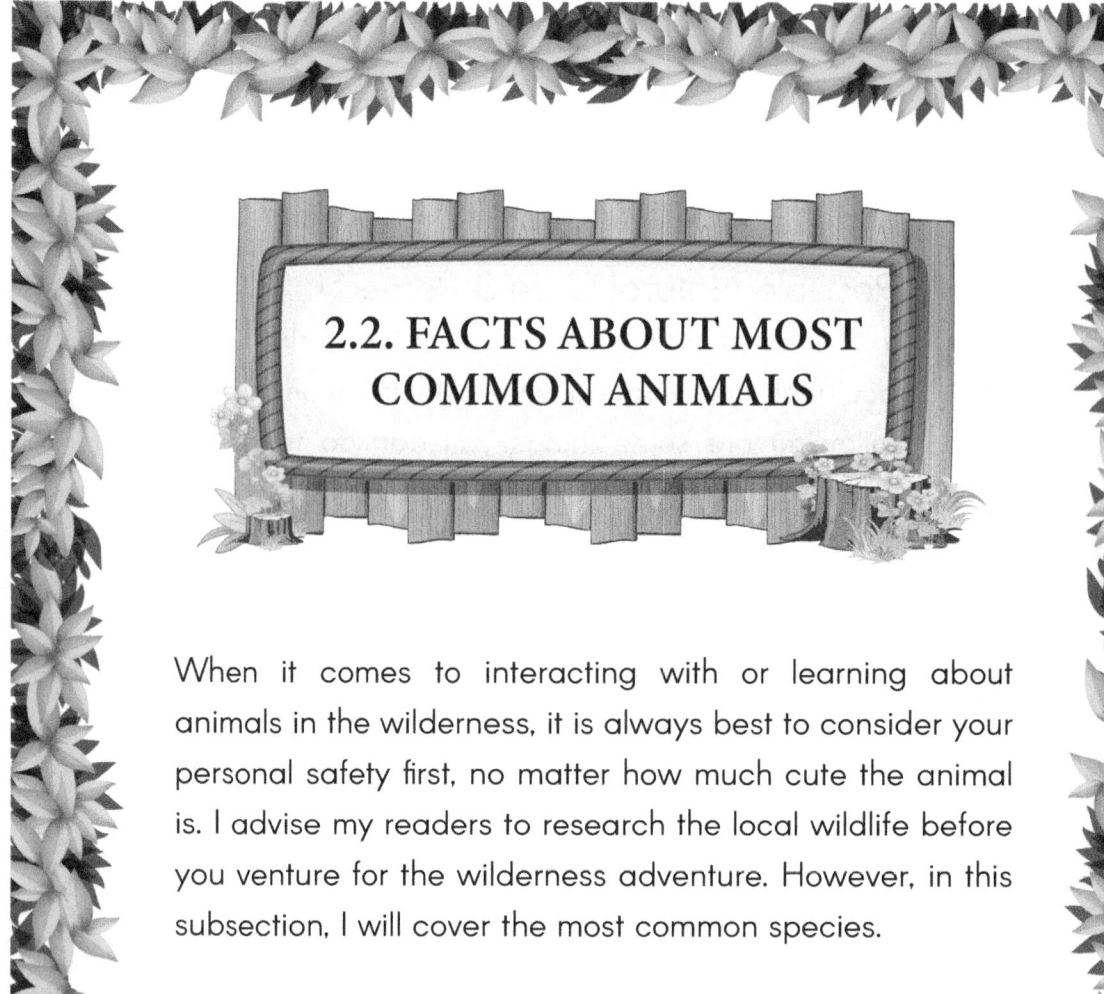

When it comes to interacting with or learning about animals in the wilderness, it is always best to consider your personal safety first, no matter how much cute the animal is. I advise my readers to research the local wildlife before you venture for the wilderness adventure. However, in this subsection, I will cover the most common species.

Bears

1. Black Bears

Humans and black bears rarely engage in social behavior. They choose to remain stealthy and are almost always observed fleeing in the event that they are observed at all; this is the most common behavior associated with them.

On the other hand, there are instances in which a hungry bear will become so desperate that it will attempt to eat a human being. In that situation, you will notice that they are rapidly approaching you without showing any sign of hesitancy.

2. Brown Bears

It is not in the nature of brown bears, sometimes known as grizzlies, to kill people for their food. On the other hand, they are possessive and protective of their territory. As a direct consequence of this, the proper response to an encounter with a grizzly bear is considerably different from how one ought to deal with a brown bear.

Wolves or Coyotes

Wolves are social carnivores that steer clear of humans because they prefer to hunt in packs. They favor deer, elk, and other large creatures more than smaller ones.

However, because wolves are susceptible to the same diseases that can affect domestic canines, there is a chance that you will come across a wolf that has become infected with rabies. Avoid coming into contact with any questionable wolves. If you have been bitten, you should see a hospital as soon as you can. In addition to the possibility that it is infected with rabies, the wolf may also be carrying other diseases that could cause an infection.

Alligators or Crocodiles

The majority of alligator assaults on humans take place in the water, which is where alligators hunt. Because you are no match for an alligator, our greatest piece of advice for dealing with these terrifying reptiles is to stay away from rivers, lakes, and ponds because they are all parts of the alligator's natural environment.

Even though alligators won't normally attack people on land, you still shouldn't let your guard down when you're in their presence. When irritated, they are capable of moving rapidly, and they do not appreciate being taunted. If you come across one basking in the sunlight, you are welcome to take pictures of it, but you should still stay your distance.

Snakes

Today, we'll learn about rattlesnakes and cottonmouths, two of the most lethal snakes in the world.

1. Rattlesnakes

Deadly rattlesnakes have an inbuilt alarm system in the form of the rattle that gives them their common name. Fortunately, we're not on these snakes' menu, so they only tend to bite when they feel threatened. Adult rattlesnakes usually only bite as a warning to people, conserving their venom for other animals. However, juveniles lack the ability to regulate their venom production; therefore, a single bite from a juvenile can cause as much damage as multiple bites from an adult. In any case, you should hurry to the hospital for treatment.

2. Cottonmouths

Like rattlesnakes, cottonmouths wait to strike until they feel threatened. However, they prefer to settle near water, so you might run into them whether you're wearing flip-flops or hiking boots. You will get bitten if you step on one. Cottonmouths don't hiss as a warning signal like rattlers do, although they do lack a warning rattle. If you look for the diamond design in brown and gold, you should be okay.

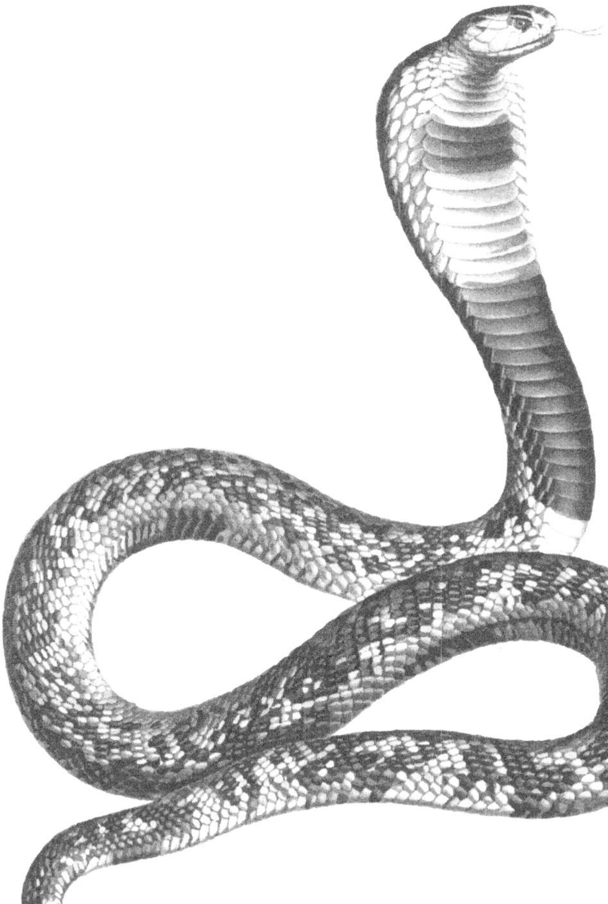

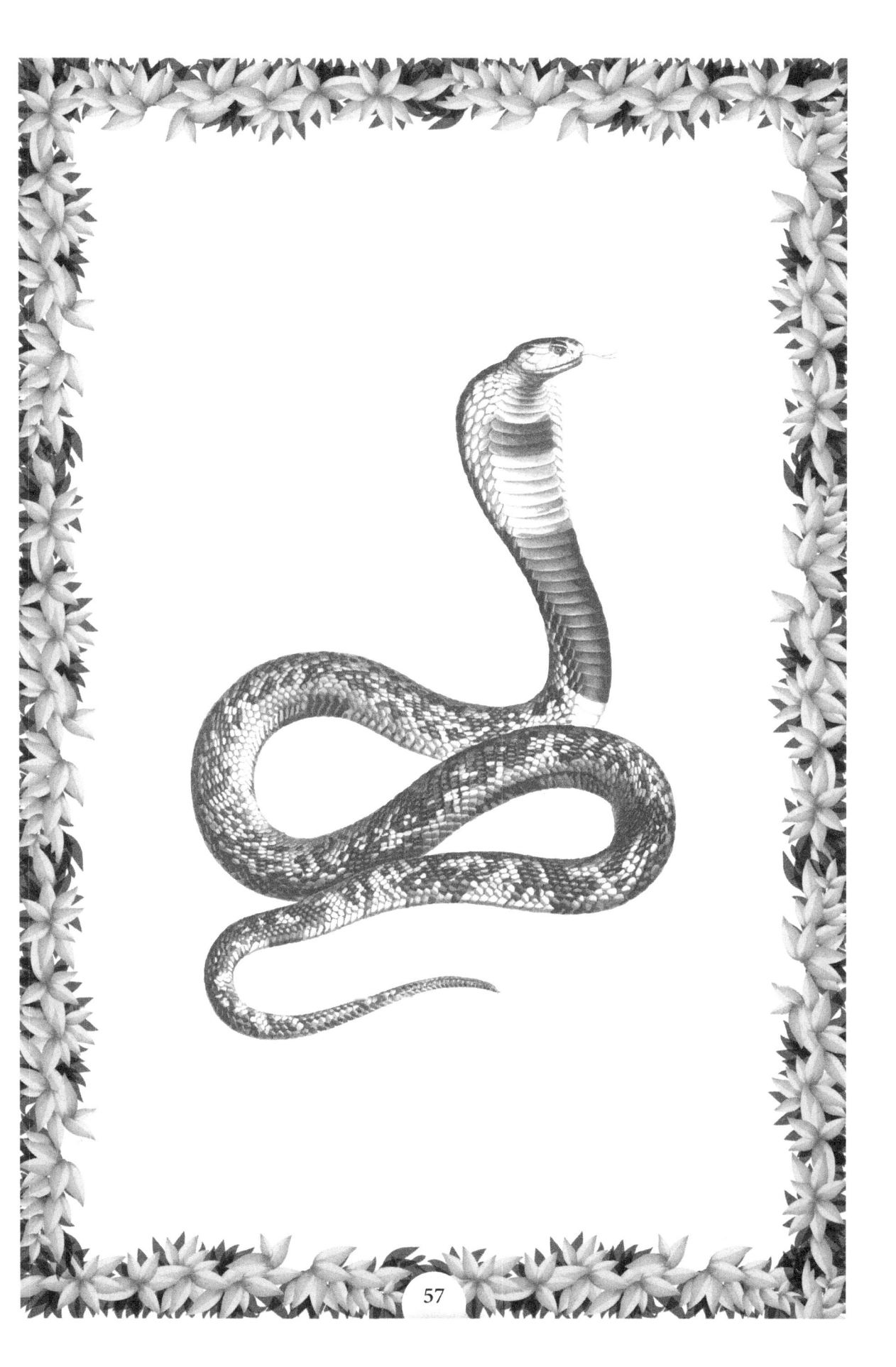

Sharks

The oceanic depths of North America are home to some of the most dangerous sharks on the entire globe. Off the coast of North America, you can find all three of the primary shark species that feed on humans.

The United States of America has been given the nickname "the shark attack capital of the world" due to the fact that it accounts for the majority of reported shark attacks around the world.

The characteristics that differentiate one species from another can change depending on where you are. Great white sharks are responsible for every fatality that has ever been recorded in the state of California. Statistics show that the bulk of attacks take place in Florida and California. On the other hand, bull sharks and tiger sharks are responsible for the majority of shark attacks in Florida.

Spiders

In North America, some of the deadliest spiders construct their webs and may creep your way in the summers.

The notorious black widow spider was one of the most dangerous species of spider until recently. Its venom was the second strongest of any spider venom, and 0.05mg of it could kill a person. From 1965 to 1990, 36 people died from Black Widow bites.

In recent years, the brown recluse spider, also known as Fiddleback, has appeared and bit victims hard.

Although not aggressive, this spider is common and has necrotic venom. While the bites are not fatal, the attacked flesh rots and recovers slowly.

Scorpions

Scorpions use their tail stinger to inject venom onto unprepared prey.

Scorpions also have pincers, but they cannot harm humans. The smaller the pincers, the greater the venom, so watch out for microscopic claws in summer.

The Arizona Bark Scorpion, the deadliest scorpion in the US, may kill with its sting. In the 1980s, over 800 Mexicans died from the scorpion's bite.

Cougars

Cougars, like black bears, are wary of humans and often avoid contact with us. Like black bears, they occasionally resort to eating humans when they are famished and desperate. Keep your eyes peeled if you find yourself in cougar territory; these cats are ambush predators and may surprise you from around a corner.

Maintain your composure if you come upon a cougar. Shout, hurl objects, and fight if you have to. If you run, you're only going to make the huge cat more predatory and increase its likelihood of chasing you.

American Bison

The American bison, at 6 feet tall and 1.5 tons in weight, is the largest land animal in the United States of America; they are only slightly smaller than the African water buffalo, which is known as the "widow maker" or "black death" due to the large number of people it kills each year.

The American bison is far more placid than its African counterpart, and will only attack if provoked; nonetheless, when angered, its impact can be devastating.

Despite their ungainly stature, American Bison are capable of speeds of up to 40 miles per hour, making a direct impact from one feel like being hit by a truck.

Deer

Even though they look like the picture of purity, deer are the deadliest animal in the United States.

More than 200 persons each year are killed by cars because deer cannot cross the road safely; in the year 2000, over 100,000 deer were killed in the United States. Authorities have adopted the abbreviation DVC (deer-vehicle collision) to describe the prevalence of incidents involving deer.

Furthermore, deer can pose a threat when found in their natural habitat, especially in the fall when stag aggression rises due to a rise in testosterone. Furthermore, springtime fawn birth is associated with increased aggression from moms who are overprotective of their young.

2.3. LOOK OUT FOR DANGERS FROM ANIMALS

BEWARE OF WILD ANIMALS

WARNING WILD ANIMALS

When Confronted By Bears

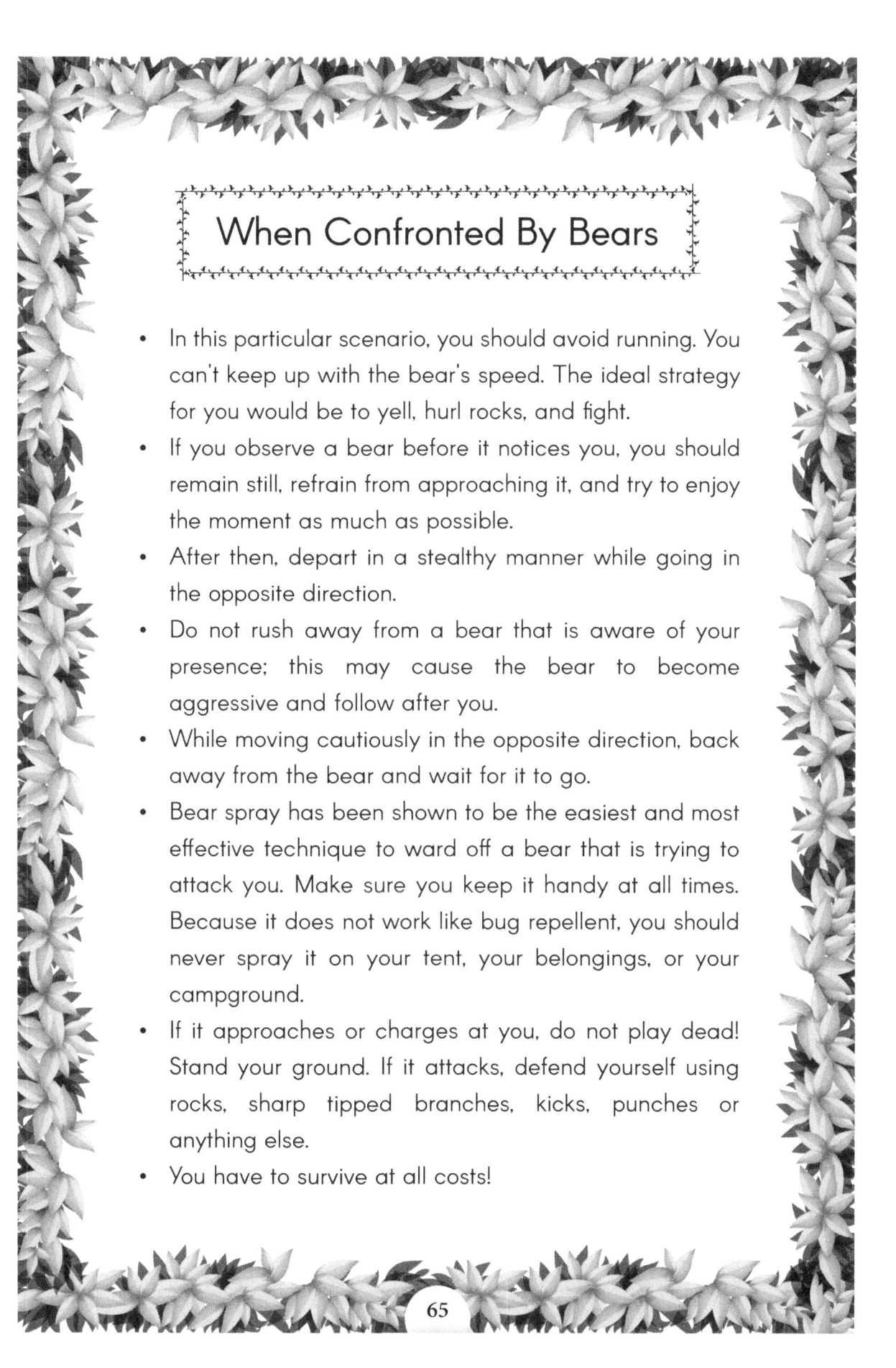

- In this particular scenario, you should avoid running. You can't keep up with the bear's speed. The ideal strategy for you would be to yell, hurl rocks, and fight.
- If you observe a bear before it notices you, you should remain still, refrain from approaching it, and try to enjoy the moment as much as possible.
- After then, depart in a stealthy manner while going in the opposite direction.
- Do not rush away from a bear that is aware of your presence; this may cause the bear to become aggressive and follow after you.
- While moving cautiously in the opposite direction, back away from the bear and wait for it to go.
- Bear spray has been shown to be the easiest and most effective technique to ward off a bear that is trying to attack you. Make sure you keep it handy at all times. Because it does not work like bug repellent, you should never spray it on your tent, your belongings, or your campground.
- If it approaches or charges at you, do not play dead! Stand your ground. If it attacks, defend yourself using rocks, sharp tipped branches, kicks, punches or anything else.
- You have to survive at all costs!

When Confronted By Cougars

- The most vital thing is to maintain as much composure as possible. Try to keep calm and not make any rash decisions.
- It's not a good idea to rush away from a cougar because of how fast they can run. Don't try to outrun them; doing so can make them chase after you.
- Don't turn your back on the cougar and don't let your eyes wander. Doing so can alert the cougar to your presence.
- Raise your arms above your head to give the illusion of a broader frame. If you can, get up on your tiptoes. Intimidating the cougar is a primary objective.
- Pronounce your words clearly and talk with an authoritative tone. Make some noise, like yelling or clapping your hands, to alert the cougar that you are human.
- Put it back slowly, while still facing the cougar, retreat. Never abandon the animal by ignoring it. It's important to keep making eye contact.
- Stand Your Ground: If the cougar comes close, don't move. Don't cower in terror or become all hunched over. Keep up the noise and make an effort to look as big and menacing as you can.

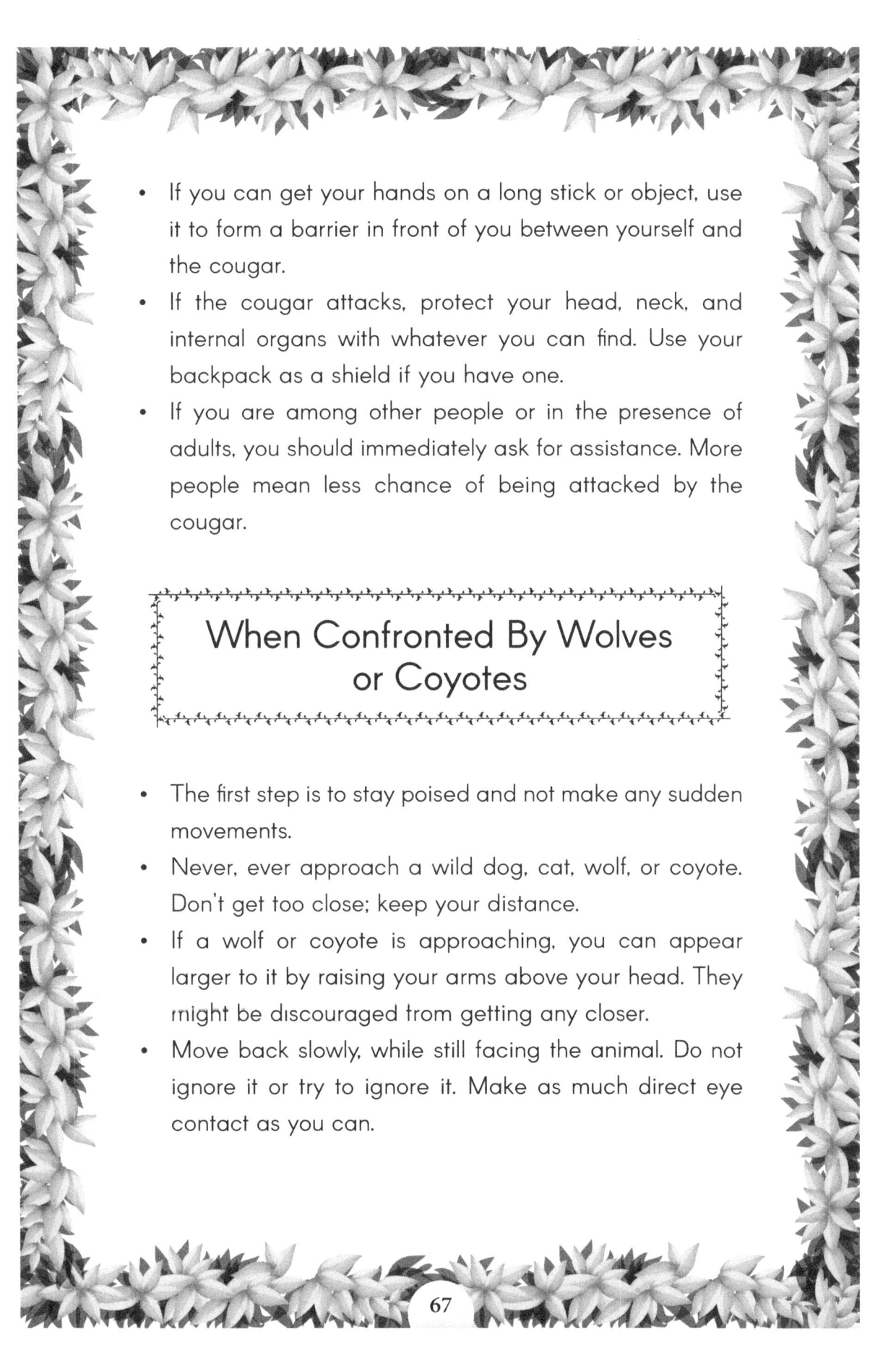

- If you can get your hands on a long stick or object, use it to form a barrier in front of you between yourself and the cougar.
- If the cougar attacks, protect your head, neck, and internal organs with whatever you can find. Use your backpack as a shield if you have one.
- If you are among other people or in the presence of adults, you should immediately ask for assistance. More people mean less chance of being attacked by the cougar.

When Confronted By Wolves or Coyotes

- The first step is to stay poised and not make any sudden movements.
- Never, ever approach a wild dog, cat, wolf, or coyote. Don't get too close; keep your distance.
- If a wolf or coyote is approaching, you can appear larger to it by raising your arms above your head. They might be discouraged from getting any closer.
- Move back slowly, while still facing the animal. Do not ignore it or try to ignore it. Make as much direct eye contact as you can.

- Warning: If you see a wolf or coyote, do not try to outrun it. If you run, you risk arousing their predatory instincts and being quickly outrun.
- Use a strong, forceful voice that conveys assurance and composure. Doing so can make the animal fearful of your presence.
- If you're able to get your hands on a long stick or other object, you can use it to put space between you and the animal.
- If a wolf or coyote were to attack, you should shield your face and neck. Roll into a ball, put your hands over your head and shoulders, and shield yourself with your rucksack or anything else you can find.
- If you are with other people or near adults, you should alert them or call for aid. They can help you scare the animal away while you run for cover.
- If you are in a group, keep as near as possible. Animals like wolves and coyotes are more wary of huge gatherings of humans.

When Confronted By Alligators or Crocodiles

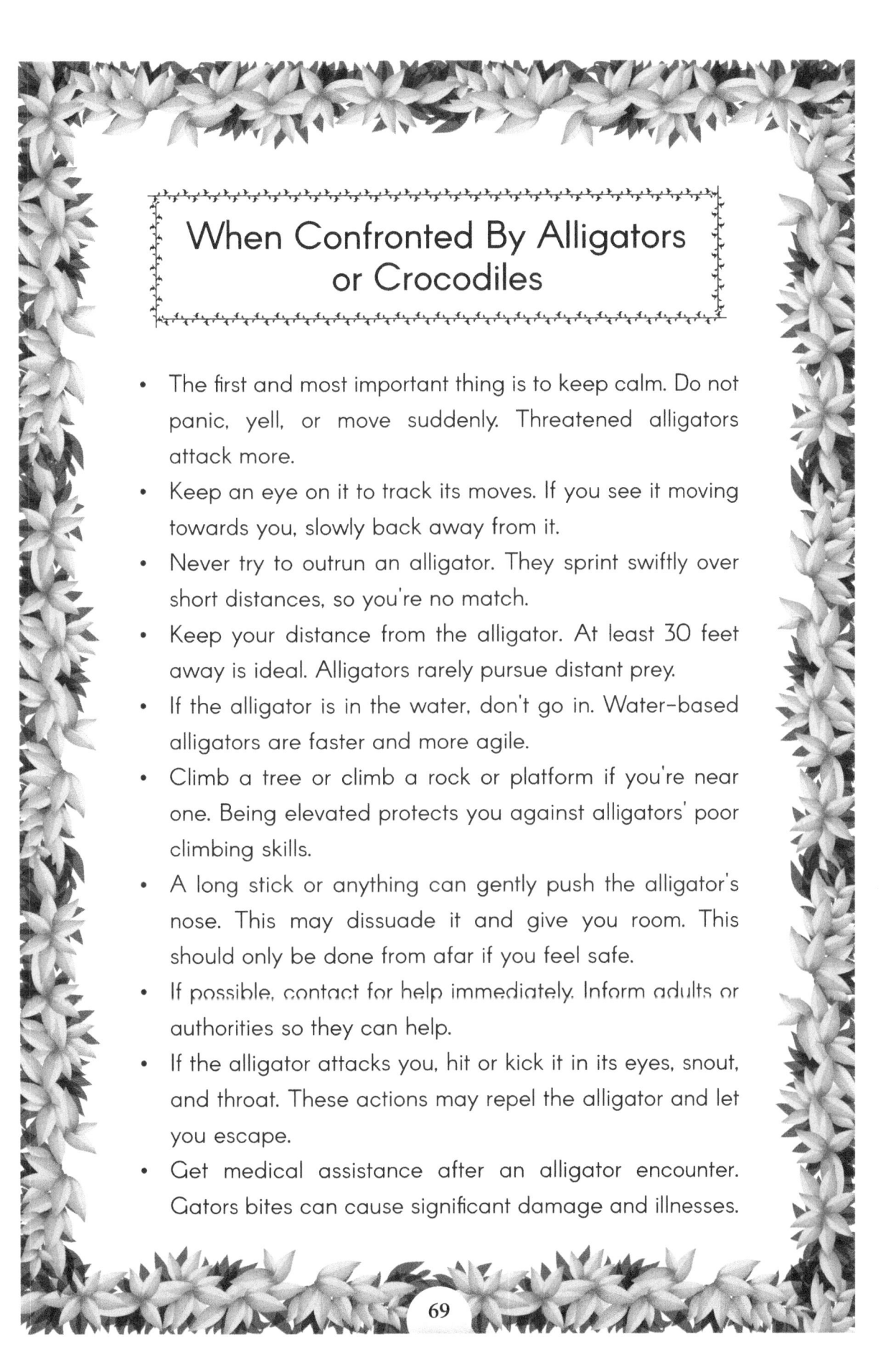

- The first and most important thing is to keep calm. Do not panic, yell, or move suddenly. Threatened alligators attack more.
- Keep an eye on it to track its moves. If you see it moving towards you, slowly back away from it.
- Never try to outrun an alligator. They sprint swiftly over short distances, so you're no match.
- Keep your distance from the alligator. At least 30 feet away is ideal. Alligators rarely pursue distant prey.
- If the alligator is in the water, don't go in. Water-based alligators are faster and more agile.
- Climb a tree or climb a rock or platform if you're near one. Being elevated protects you against alligators' poor climbing skills.
- A long stick or anything can gently push the alligator's nose. This may dissuade it and give you room. This should only be done from afar if you feel safe.
- If possible, contact for help immediately. Inform adults or authorities so they can help.
- If the alligator attacks you, hit or kick it in its eyes, snout, and throat. These actions may repel the alligator and let you escape.
- Get medical assistance after an alligator encounter. Gators bites can cause significant damage and illnesses.

When Confronted By Snakes

- The first and most important thing is to keep calm. Snakes rarely attack unless threatened.
- Stop immediately. Snakes detect prey and hazards mostly through movement and vibration. Standing still reduces visibility.
- Even if the snake appears harmless, never touch or approach it. Some venomous snakes look like non-venomous ones, making identification difficult.
- Retreat and cautiously move away from the snake. Go the other way from the snake.
- Stay away from the snake. At least 6 feet is advised. Most snakes can attack short distances, so allow them room.
- Do not run from the snake. Fast snakes may chase when running.
- Gently prod the snake from afar to get it to go. The idea is to create space, not hurt the snake.
- While withdrawing, be mindful of your surroundings. Avoid treading on snakes and other risks.
- If in a group or near adults, call for aid. They can guide you away from the snake safely.
- Even if you're not convinced the snake is dangerous, get medical assistance if it bites you. First aid treatments include immobilizing the bitten area below heart level while waiting for help.

When Confronted By Sharks

- The most important thing to remember when confronted by a shark is to stay calm. Worsening the situation by panicking is possible.
- Keep Staring at the Shark: Make sure you maintain eye contact with the shark . In certain circumstances, this may cause them to retreat.
- Never turn your back on the shark; always maintain eye contact. If sharks lose track of you, they are more likely to sneak up on you from behind.
- If the shark is close but not aggressively pursuing you, you should begin backing away gently while keeping eye contact with it as much as possible.
- Do not make any rapid movements, and avoid splashing around. The shark may become interested in you if you move quickly.
- If you're swimming or otherwise in the water, maintain as much of a vertical position as feasible. In the eyes of the shark, you will look like less of a meal this way.
- If you can see the coast, swim back to it gently and quietly; don't panic. Those on boats should immediately abandon ship.
- If you have access to a buoy or other floating object, use it to establish a barrier between yourself and the shark.

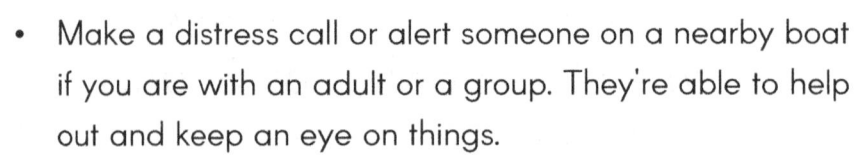

- Make a distress call or alert someone on a nearby boat if you are with an adult or a group. They're able to help out and keep an eye on things.
- If the shark does get hostile and tries to attack, you can defend yourself by striking at its weak spots, such as its eyes, gills, or nose. Make weapons out of everything you can find, like a camera or snorkeling equipment.

When Confronted By Spiders

- The most crucial step is to maintain composure. Keep in mind that most spiders are completely harmless to humans.
- Don't freak out and start yelling or making frantic gestures. Fear causes the spider to flinch, which can provoke an attack.
- Don't touch the spider or try to pick it up. Avoid getting too close.
- If you must gaze at the spider, please do it from a distance. Make use of your sight, but don't encroach.
- If a spider is near you and you feel uneasy, slowly back away until you have some distance between you.
- If the spider is not in close proximity to you and is not making any hostile moves toward you, then you can relax and let it go about its business. In general, spiders are less curious about people and more focused in finding a meal or a mate.

- You can use a long stick or something to gently steer the spider away from your campsite or personal space if you need to do so.
- Avoid killing or hurting the spider unless necessary (this is extremely unusual). Insect populations are kept in check thanks to spiders, which play a crucial role in ecosystems.
- Protect yourself from spider bites by donning long sleeves, pants, and shoes with closed toes if you happen to be in a region where such creatures are common.
- Always wash your hands after being outside, as this will help get rid of any bugs or spiders that may have gotten on them.

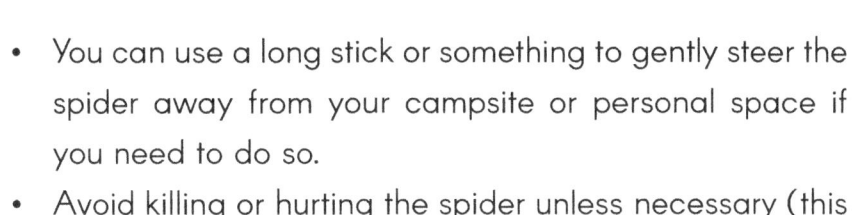

When Confronted By Scorpions

- Keep in mind that several species of scorpions are not lethal to humans. So, try to stay calm when you see a scorpion.
- Don't freak out and start yelling or making frantic gestures. If you panic, the scorpion may be startled and sting you unnecessarily.
- Never, ever try to pick up or otherwise handle the scorpion. Avoid getting too close.
- Look at the scorpion from a distance if you must see it up close. Make use of your sight, but don't encroach.

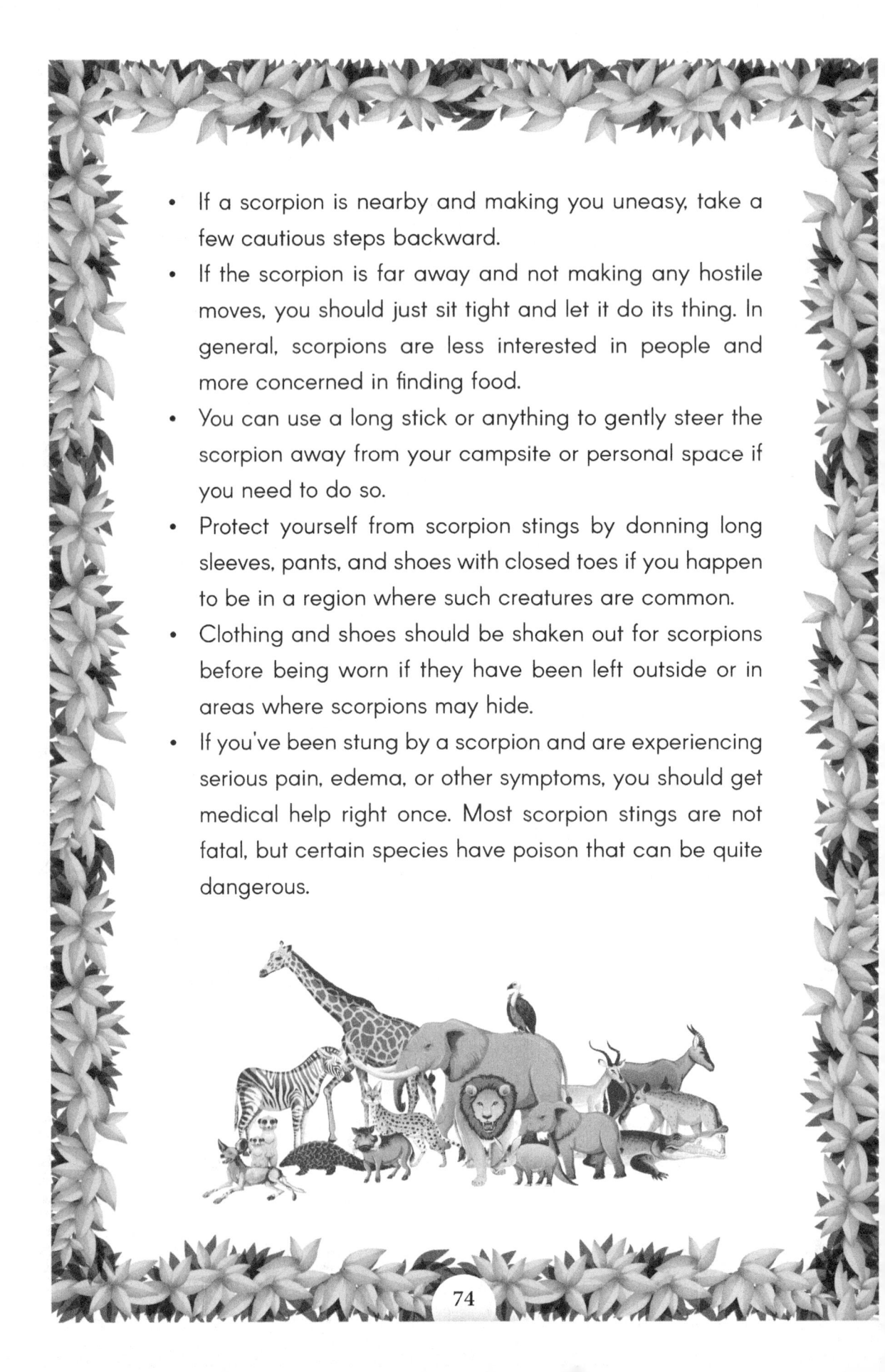

- If a scorpion is nearby and making you uneasy, take a few cautious steps backward.
- If the scorpion is far away and not making any hostile moves, you should just sit tight and let it do its thing. In general, scorpions are less interested in people and more concerned in finding food.
- You can use a long stick or anything to gently steer the scorpion away from your campsite or personal space if you need to do so.
- Protect yourself from scorpion stings by donning long sleeves, pants, and shoes with closed toes if you happen to be in a region where such creatures are common.
- Clothing and shoes should be shaken out for scorpions before being worn if they have been left outside or in areas where scorpions may hide.
- If you've been stung by a scorpion and are experiencing serious pain, edema, or other symptoms, you should get medical help right once. Most scorpion stings are not fatal, but certain species have poison that can be quite dangerous.

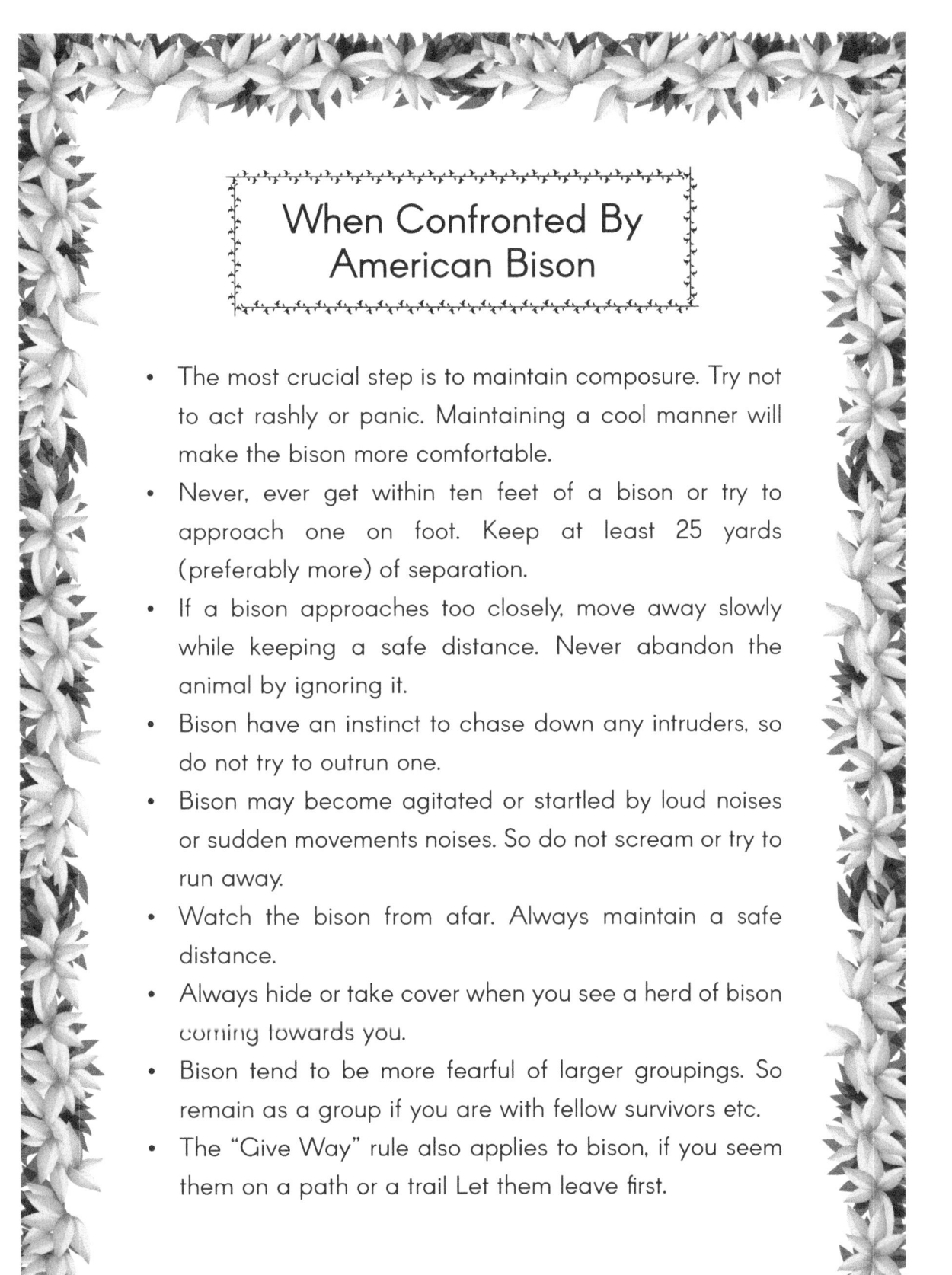

When Confronted By American Bison

- The most crucial step is to maintain composure. Try not to act rashly or panic. Maintaining a cool manner will make the bison more comfortable.
- Never, ever get within ten feet of a bison or try to approach one on foot. Keep at least 25 yards (preferably more) of separation.
- If a bison approaches too closely, move away slowly while keeping a safe distance. Never abandon the animal by ignoring it.
- Bison have an instinct to chase down any intruders, so do not try to outrun one.
- Bison may become agitated or startled by loud noises or sudden movements noises. So do not scream or try to run away.
- Watch the bison from afar. Always maintain a safe distance.
- Always hide or take cover when you see a herd of bison coming towards you.
- Bison tend to be more fearful of larger groupings. So remain as a group if you are with fellow survivors etc.
- The "Give Way" rule also applies to bison, if you seem them on a path or a trail Let them leave first.

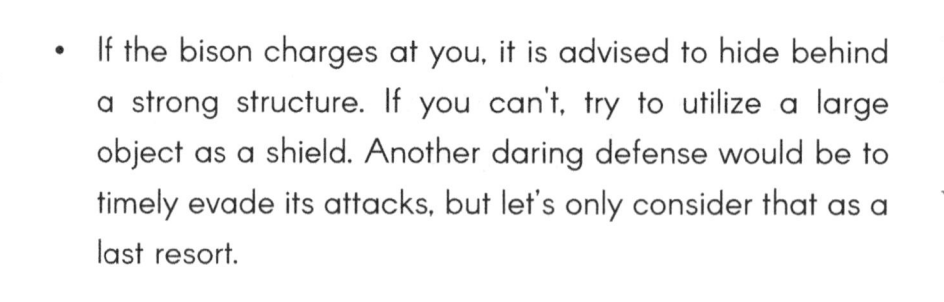

- If the bison charges at you, it is advised to hide behind a strong structure. If you can't, try to utilize a large object as a shield. Another daring defense would be to timely evade its attacks, but let's only consider that as a last resort.

When Confronted By Deer

- In most cases, deer won't attack a human if they see one. So, no need to be afraid and run away.
- Never try to approach a deer or get any closer than you have to. Keep at least 50 yards of distance between you and the threat.
- The best way to see deer is to move slowly and softly. Try not to make any unexpected noises or movements.
- Deer should not be pursued or cornered. If it feels threatened, it will be able to flee.
- Give deer the right way if you encounter one on a trail or sidewalk. The deer must be given the space to escape from you at its own pace.
- Don't yell or make any other distracting noises. This is good for both you and the deer since it keeps the peace.
- Avoid making direct eye contact with a deer, as this may be perceived as aggressive behavior. Keep your gaze down.

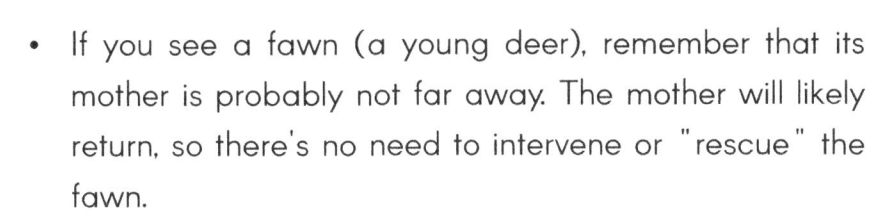

- If you see a fawn (a young deer), remember that its mother is probably not far away. The mother will likely return, so there's no need to intervene or "rescue" the fawn.
- Deer should not be offered any kind of food. Wild animals' normal diets and behaviors can be thrown off by human intervention.
- Always keep safety in the forefront of your mind while driving, but especially in places where deer are prevalent, and especially at dawn and dusk, when they are most active. Take it easy; there may be deer crossing the road.

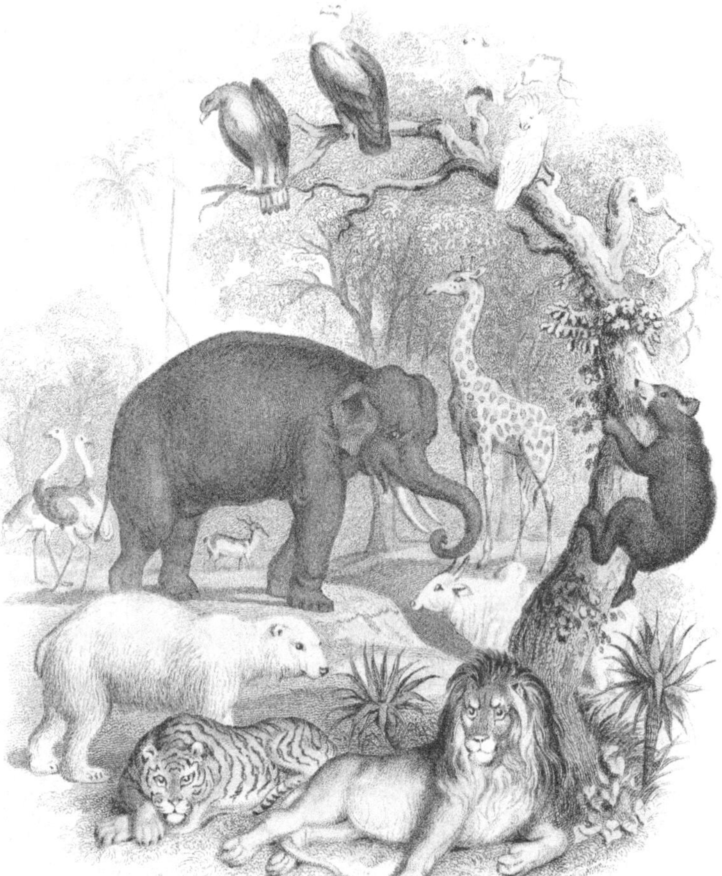

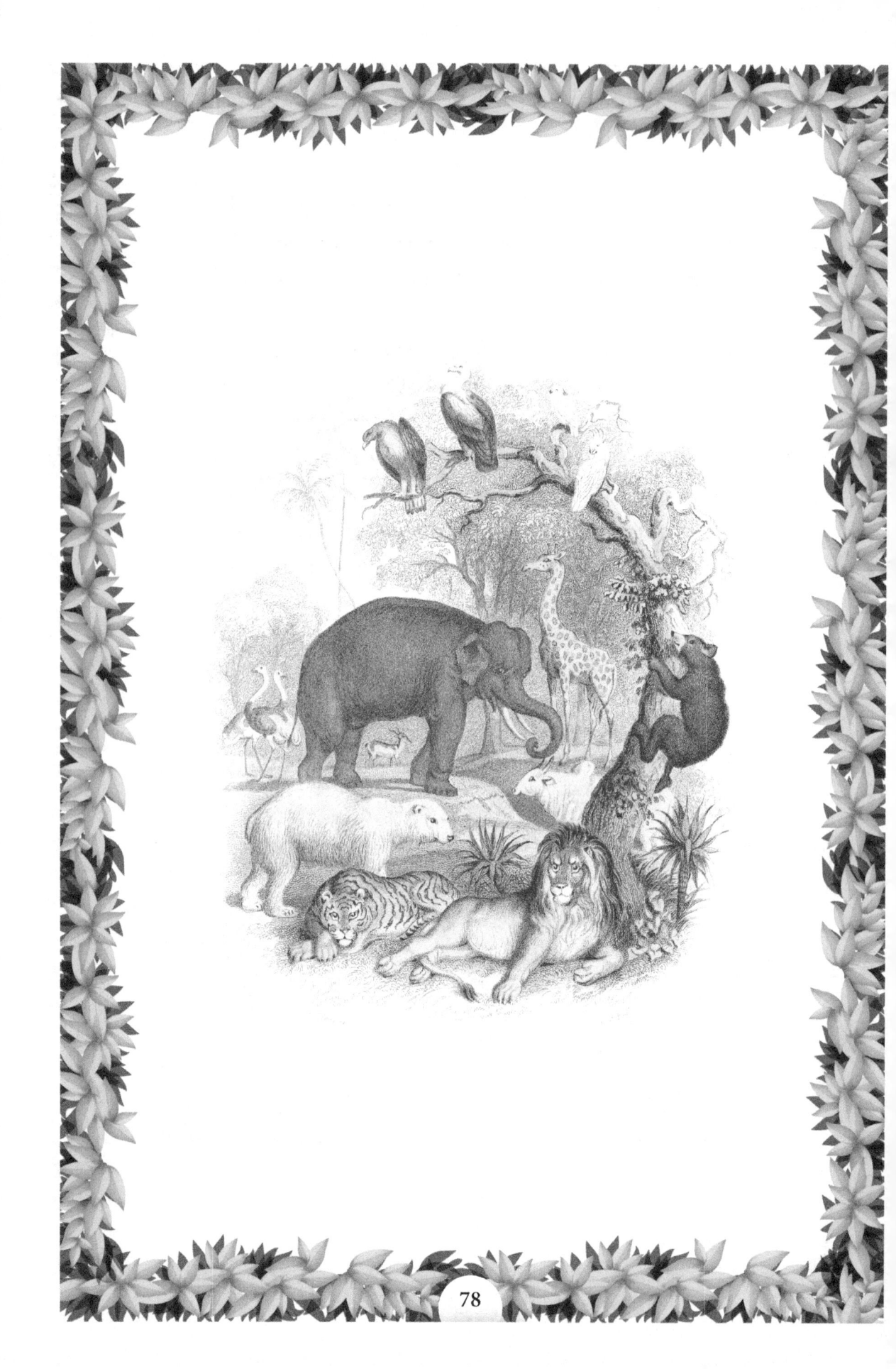

PART 3
INVENTORY SKILLS

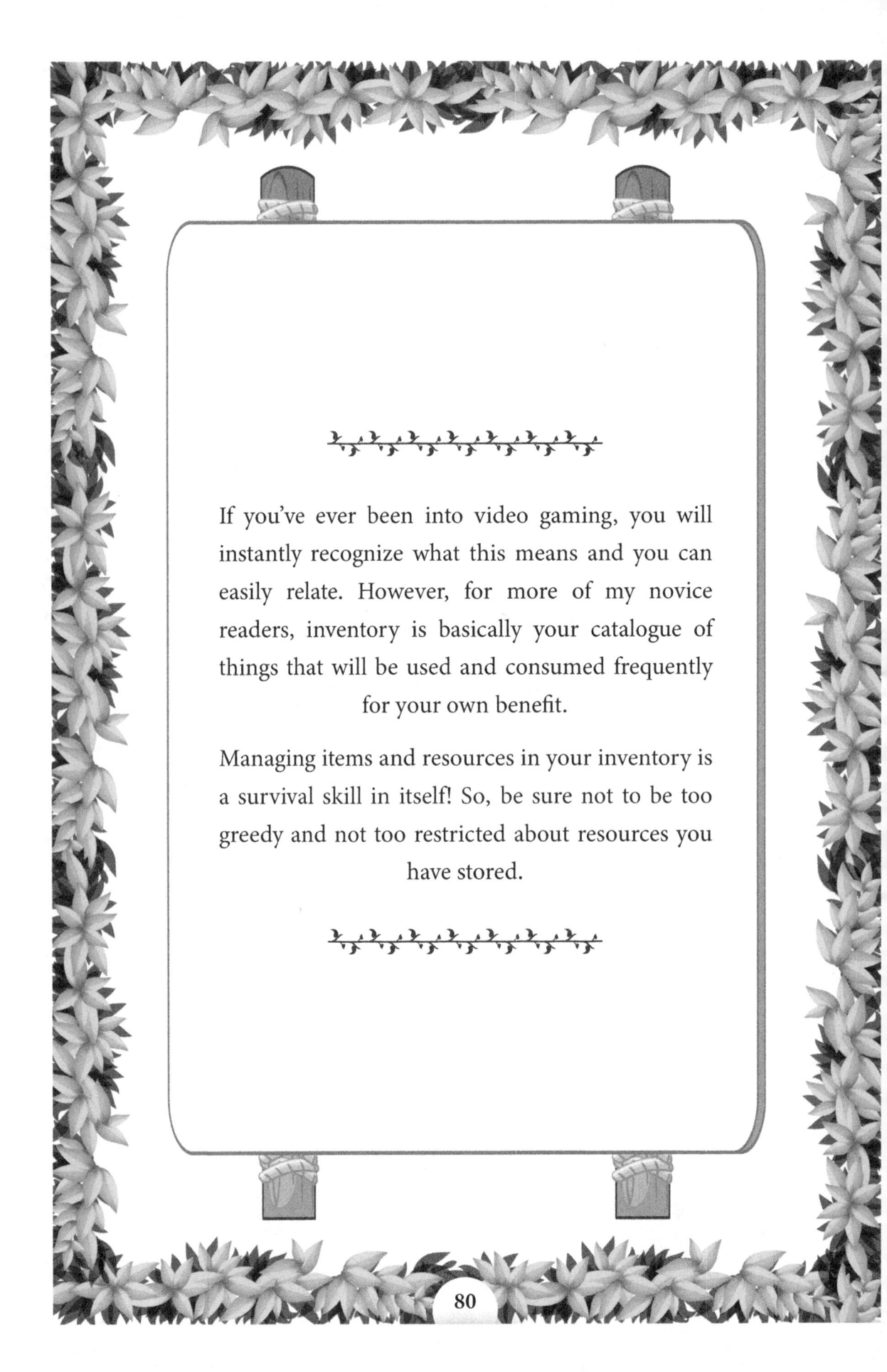

If you've ever been into video gaming, you will instantly recognize what this means and you can easily relate. However, for more of my novice readers, inventory is basically your catalogue of things that will be used and consumed frequently for your own benefit.

Managing items and resources in your inventory is a survival skill in itself! So, be sure not to be too greedy and not too restricted about resources you have stored.

SURVIVAL KIT B RESOURCING FOOD & WATER

After identifying, what's dangerous in your environment and how to avoid it. We will move on to the next phase; which starts with basic strategies to acquire natural resources such food and water.

Water and food are the two most vital resources for the basic survival of humans. You may go only a few days without food, but cannot go without water for more than 24 hours. So, whenever you are stranded alone in the wilderness, it is absolutely necessary that you find these resources and store them and use them effectively during your survival days and this chapter will help you in learning just that.

3.1. FORAGING & COOKING FOOD

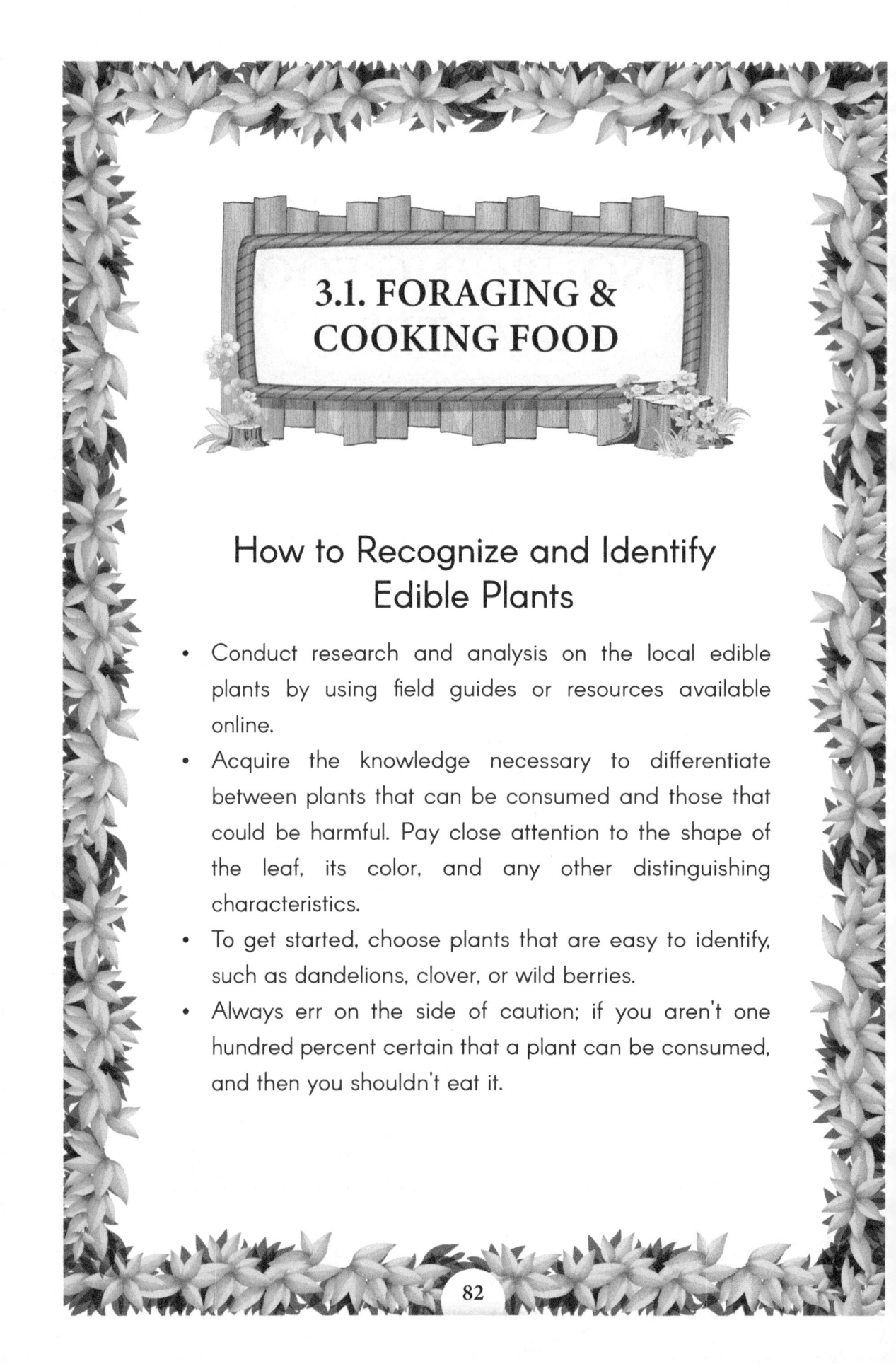

How to Recognize and Identify Edible Plants

- Conduct research and analysis on the local edible plants by using field guides or resources available online.
- Acquire the knowledge necessary to differentiate between plants that can be consumed and those that could be harmful. Pay close attention to the shape of the leaf, its color, and any other distinguishing characteristics.
- To get started, choose plants that are easy to identify, such as dandelions, clover, or wild berries.
- Always err on the side of caution; if you aren't one hundred percent certain that a plant can be consumed, and then you shouldn't eat it.

Basic Hunting Techniques

- Construct simple snares making use of natural elements such as sticks and vines.
- Learn how to track animals by examining for indications left behind by them such as footprints, droppings, and foliage that has been chewed on.
- When hunting birds or smaller wildlife, patience and subtlety are essential skills to have.

An Introduction to Fishing

- Construct your own fishing equipment out of common household objects such as twine, hooks, and bait.
- Find places that are likely to have fish, such as rivers, ponds, or the coastline.
- Gain experience in fundamental aspects of fishing, such as how to cast a line and set up a fishing pole.

Methods Used in the Earliest Forms of Cooking

- Create a fire in your campsite by utilizing tinder and dry, dead wood.
- Makeshift barbecues can be created by skewering food items onto sticks and placing them on flat rocks.
- Experiment with a variety of cooking techniques, changing the distance from the fire in order to achieve the desired temperature.

3.2. FOOD MANAGEMENT

Techniques for the Preserving of Food

- Hanging meat over a smokey fire allows it to dry out and become more shelf-stable.
- The best way to dry fruits, vegetables, or meat is to slice it into thin strips and either let it air dry or put it in the sun.
- The process of fermenting vegetables in a saltwater brine can result in the creation of sauerkraut or kimchi.

Environment Friendly Food Disposal Methods

- Burying food scraps in holes that are at least 6 to 8 inches deep so as not to attract wild animals.
- Disperse leftover food scraps away from your campground in order to get rid of the odor.
- To reduce the amount of waste produced, try to always use containers that can be reused.

Putting Every Non-Reusable Component To Use

- When developing recipes, try to think of ways to employ every component of the animal or plant.
- Make soup out of the bones, or use them to build various things.
- Create items of clothes and coverings for shelters out of animal hides, if available or you can procure any.
- Nothing that is expected to get bad or be unusable alter should be stored. All such things should be used completely in the moment.

3.3. WATER RESOURCES & STORAGE

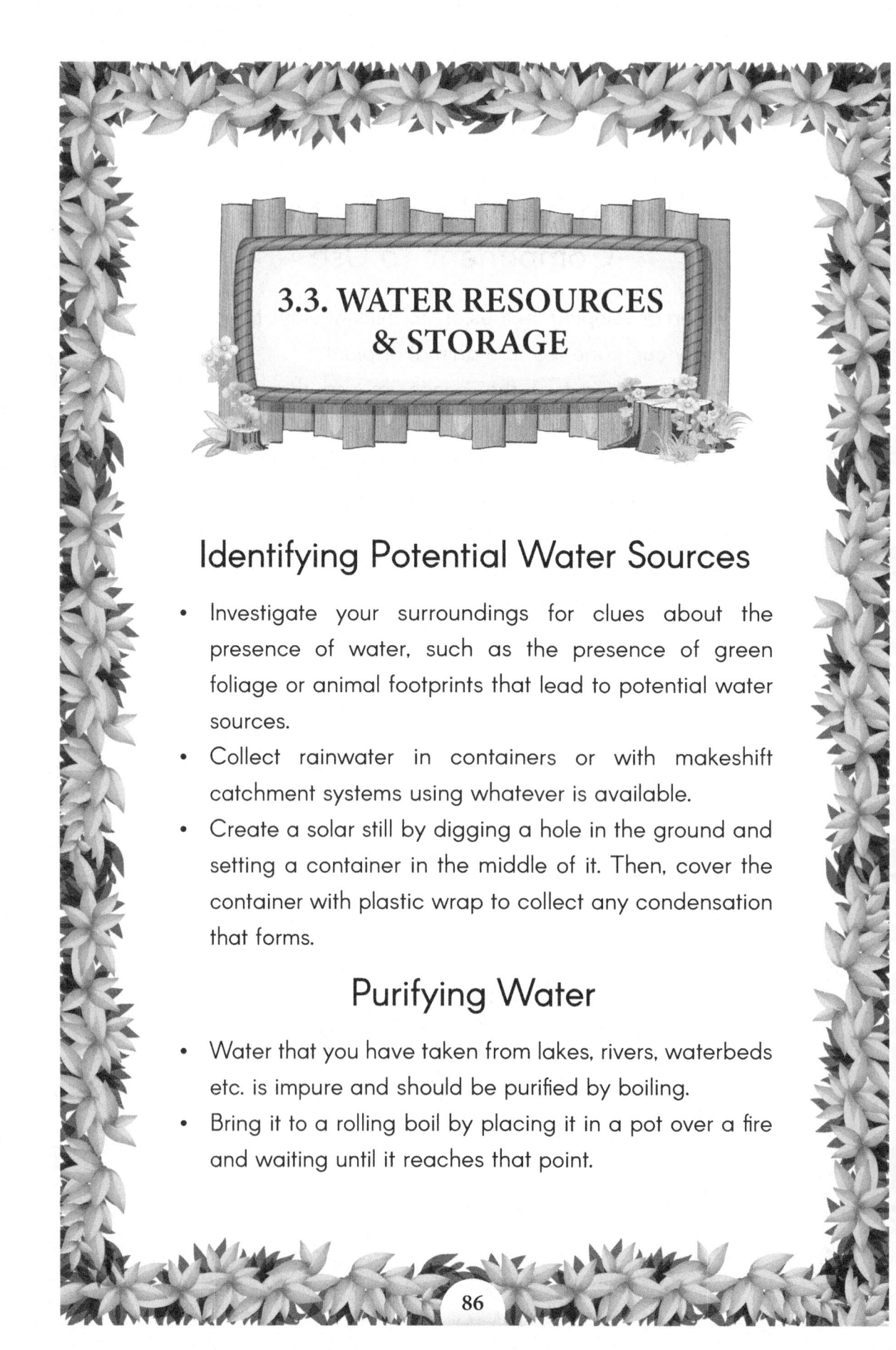

Identifying Potential Water Sources

- Investigate your surroundings for clues about the presence of water, such as the presence of green foliage or animal footprints that lead to potential water sources.
- Collect rainwater in containers or with makeshift catchment systems using whatever is available.
- Create a solar still by digging a hole in the ground and setting a container in the middle of it. Then, cover the container with plastic wrap to collect any condensation that forms.

Purifying Water

- Water that you have taken from lakes, rivers, waterbeds etc. is impure and should be purified by boiling.
- Bring it to a rolling boil by placing it in a pot over a fire and waiting until it reaches that point.

- Sand, charcoal, and linen are some examples of natural filtration materials that can be used to filter water.
- If you have access to water purification tablets or drops, you should think about utilizing them.

Storage of Water

- It is important to store water in clean containers with lids that fit securely so that it does not become contaminated.
- It is best to keep water containers off the ground so that they do not come into contact with dirt or insects.
- You can use bowl shaped natural elements, such as half-cut dry, clean coconuts or pouches and flasks made from clean and dry animal hides, in case any other container is not available.

Mastering these abilities calls for time and expertise. If you intend to rely on your survival abilities in the bush, it is crucial that you acquire more knowledge in this area before setting off on your journey.

IN THE WILD ABYSS

The Extraordinary Story of a Teenager's Fight for Survival in the Woods

It is a survival story that takes place in a thick, dense forest deep in the middle of the Appalachian Mountains. The survivalist is Jake Williams, a 16-year-old young man who faced the adversity of living alone in the wilderness for two weeks. He accidentally got misled from the map due to a minor reading error. But luckily, being a scout in his pre-teen years, he had some knowledge of camping and basic first aid. The next, he had to improvise and further survive, and today you have his story!

A Person Who Enjoys Being in the Wild

Jake was very comfortable in natural environments. Since he came from a family that spent a lot of time outside (hiking and camping), he learned a lot about those activities at an early age and became very skilled in them. He was taught by his parents how to find his way about in the bush, construct shelters, and make fires; these were fundamental abilities that would prove to be quite useful in the future.

The Misfortunate Outing Spent Camping

Jake made the decision to go on a solitary camping trip in the middle of the summer to get away from it all and experience the peace and quiet that can only be found in the outdoors. He started out his journey with a sense of youthful enthusiasm, carrying a rucksack full of camping supplies and a notebook that was written in with advice from his loved ones.

A Startling Reversal of Fortune

Jake's vacation to the woods for some camping turned into a dangerous adventure when he got lost in the thick of the forest and became disoriented. It would have been easy for him to give in to a state of panic, but he recalled the instructions that his family had given him regarding how to maintain composure in dangerous situations. He stopped for a second and took a slow, deep breath to compose himself before continuing. After that, he took the time to closely analyze his surroundings and reflect on the challenging circumstances he found himself in.

Abilities in Constructing Shelters

Jake was well aware that constructing a shelter was the first thing that needed to be done in order to protect himself from the elements. He took great care in selecting a site that would be appropriate for his hideout, and he gathered all of the components he would need, including twigs, leaves, and vines. He relied heavily on the information and abilities that he had gained throughout his time spent surviving in the bush. He protected himself from the elements by constructing a lean-to-style shelter that was robust and impervious to water. This provided him with a safe haven.

The Value of Being Able to Use Fire

After ensuring that he had a safe location to sleep, Jake turned his attention to devising a method through which he might produce heat and light. He wanted it to be useful in a variety of contexts, such as in the kitchen and for calling for assistance. He managed to light a fire successfully by using the fire starter and dry tinder that he had brought with him. This enabled him to ensure that he would not perish during the chilly and wet woodland nights.

Obtaining Sources of Water

Jake was aware of how critical it was to maintain a healthy level of hydration at all times, especially when they were fighting for their lives. He used a variety of techniques to gather water from surrounding streams and rain and purify it so that he would always have a supply of clean water for drinking. Consequently, he never ran out of fresh water.

Looking for Food in the Wild

Jake was able to keep himself alive thanks to his talents as a forager because he was aware that food would be difficult to come by in the woods. He took great care in determining which plants, berries, and fungi were edible, and he routinely verified his understanding to steer clear of any potentially hazardous ingredients.

The Strength to Thrive in Isolation

Jake was forced to confront the horrible reality of his solitude and loneliness as the days went into weeks. He would write in his notebook to break up the monotony of the alone he felt by recording his experiences, ideas, and observations. He also sang songs and conversed with the forest critters that eventually became his friends, and he found comfort in the company of their presence.

Sending an SOS for Assistance

Jake was fully aware that sending out a distress signal would give him the best possible chance of being rescued. He utilized a mirror that was part of his camping kit to reflect sunlight in the hopes that someone walking by would notice the glimmer and inquire about what was going on. In addition to this, he constructed a massive "SOS" sign on the ground of the forest using rocks and logs so that it would be visible from the air in the event that a search and rescue team was dispatched.

Encounters of Personal Nature with Wild Animals

During the course of his ordeal, Jake came into contact with a number of animals that made their home in the forest, such as raccoons, squirrels, and deer. His knowledge of the local species allowed him to coexist quietly with them, and he had the good sense to hide his food so as not to attract larger, potentially deadly animals.

The Extraordinary Deliverance

A fortunate break came Jake's way on the fourteenth day of the hardship he was through in the forest. Hikers came upon his SOS sign by accident and alerted the authorities as soon as they could after seeing it. Teams trained in search and rescue operations have been sent to his position. After weathering the dangers of the wilderness by himself, Jake, who was injured but still alive, was thrilled to come across other humans.

Life After Struggle for Continuity

The incredible account of Jake's escape from certain death has served as a motivational tool for readers all around the world. His family, who had been going crazy with concern, wept tears of relief and joy as they welcomed his safe homecoming after he had been missing for a long time. Jake's camping and survival abilities, which he had polished through the years of family vacations, had surely played a significant impact on his capacity to endure the hardships that he faced in the forest.

Lessons Learned from a Survivor Who Is Only 16 Years Old

In spite of the challenges he faced, Jake was able to overcome those obstacles. Thanks to his intelligence, flexibility, and drive. It serves as a useful reminder that preparedness and outdoor abilities can make a world of difference in the event that one must rely on survival techniques. His astounding narrative of survival is a potent representation of the power of the human spirit and the resiliency that can be discovered even in the most terrible of circumstances.

Nowadays…

Jake Williams has never stopped following his enthusiasm for the great outdoors, and he does so with a deeper understanding of the natural environment as well as a real respect for the strength and unpredictability of the wilderness. To this day, Jake Williams never quits pursuing his passion for the great outdoors. When confronted with the hardships that the great outdoors presents, his story stands as an enduring monument to the incredible things that are possible to accomplish with resourcefulness, tenacity, and a mindset that never gives up.

PART 4
BUILDING SKILLS

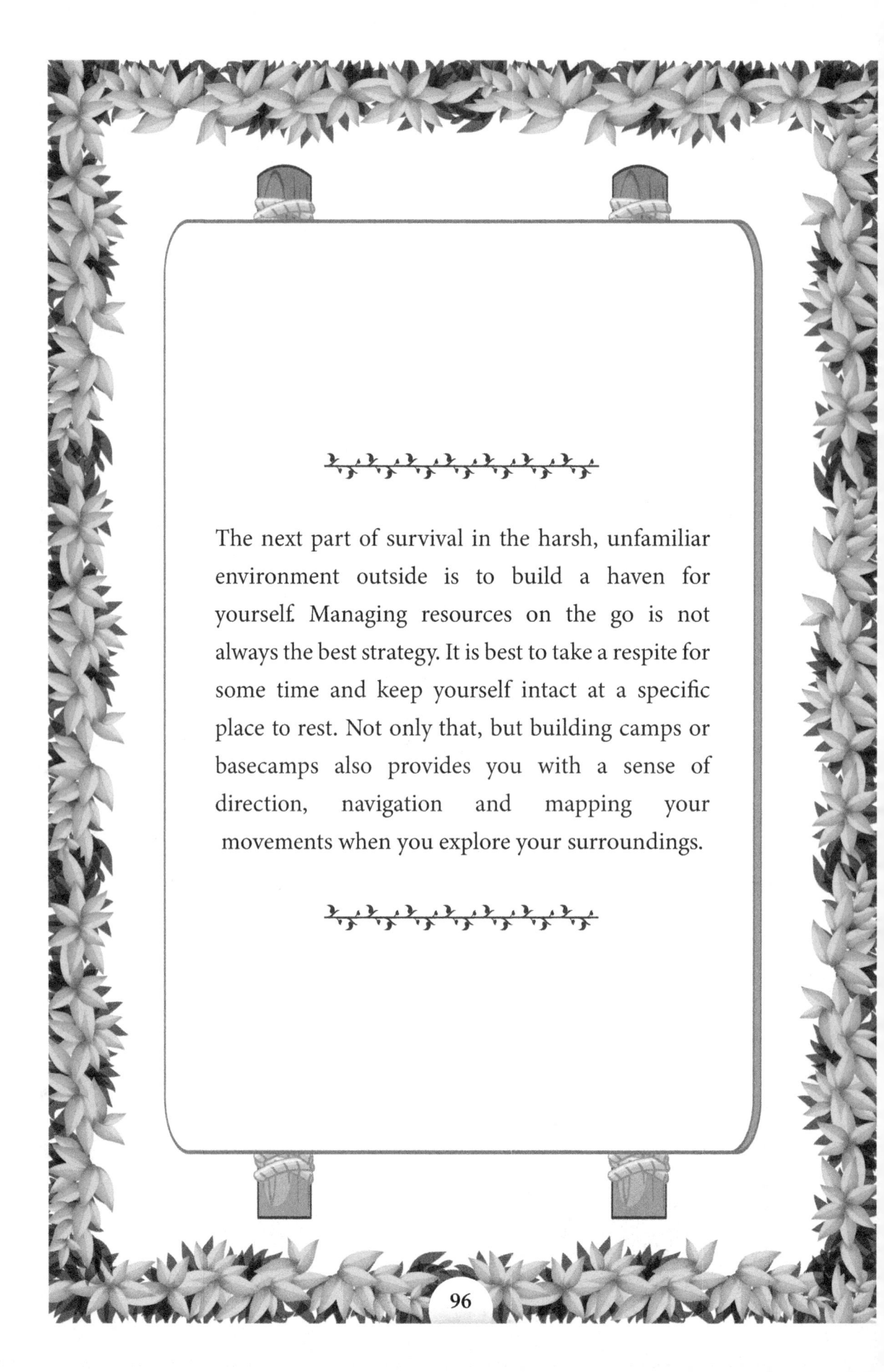

The next part of survival in the harsh, unfamiliar environment outside is to build a haven for yourself. Managing resources on the go is not always the best strategy. It is best to take a respite for some time and keep yourself intact at a specific place to rest. Not only that, but building camps or basecamps also provides you with a sense of direction, navigation and mapping your movements when you explore your surroundings.

SURVIVAL KIT C CREATING YOUR BASECAMP

Resources and your big-self have to go somewhere, right? That's where camps or basecamps come into the picture. Having a roof over your head is indeed a blessing. But what happens when you don't? Simple, survival expects you to build one for your safety, if not, comfort.

Building a suitable shelter is very important for your survival in the wilderness, think of it as storing yourself away in a specific space in order to keep yourself from harm and extreme weather.

4.1. GATHERING IMPORTANT RESOURCES

In order to construct a proper basecamp, it is necessary that you gather the proper materials. The tips on this step are given below:

- Choosing an Appropriate Place: Before collecting materials, first select an appropriate spot for your basecamp. Look for a level place that is slightly raised that is not near any potential dangers such as animal tracks or flood zones
- Gathering Items: Vines, branches, leaves, logs are the most commonly used materials in construction of a basecamp. These items can be used in different combinations to build the type of basecamp that best suits you.
- Collecting Firewood: It is important to additionally collect firewood while you are gathering other things. This will serve two purposes: one, it will provide warmth, and second, it will help to prevent wildlife.

- Access To Water Source: Ensure that your basecamp is situated in close proximity to a water source, but not so close that it will be flooded in the event of precipitation. Clean water is absolutely necessary for life.
- Medical Supplies: An easily accessible and well-stocked first aid kit. This includes common bandages and antiseptics along with any and all personal prescriptions. This is a vital thing to have at your basecamp.
- Emergency Signaling: Signaling equipment such as flares, whistles, flash torches, mirrors or a lantern with extra batteries should always be at your basecamp.

4.2. HOW TO SET UP CAMP

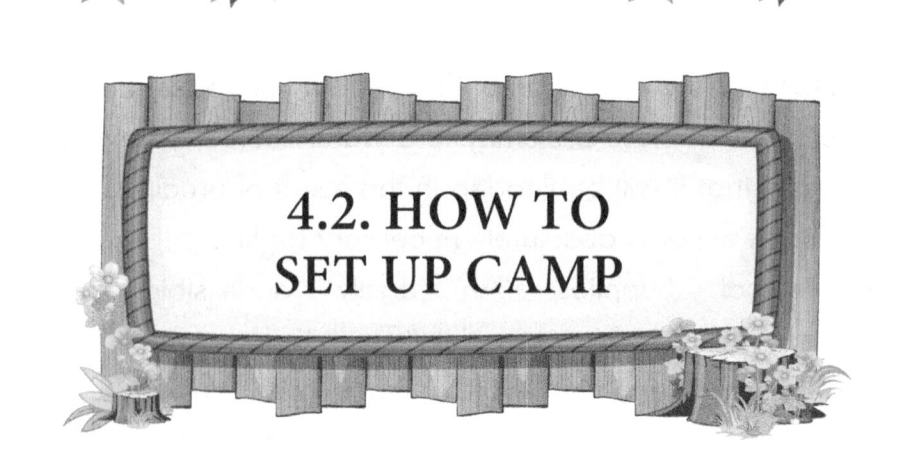

Once you have collected all the required supplies and materials, it's time to start building your basecamp. This will provide you with a safe and secure place to take shelter.

- Constructing a Shelter: With the materials accessible to you. The following three types of shelters are all common choices in this category.

1. Sloped Roof or Lean-To Shelter:

- A primary support beam is needed first. This should be a long, robust branch.
- Then lean smaller branches against it to create a diagonal, sloping roof.
- To cover the roof, pines, leaves, needles or a tarp should be used.
- This type of shelter is best for areas with a harsh or unfavorable weather.

2. Double Sloped Roof or A-Frame Shelter:

- Take four long branches or logs and form the letter "A" with them.
- Set one set at the front and one at the back.
- Add one additional long beam on the upper side as a total support connecting the two frames.
- The remaining frame areas should be secured at the top, and the frame should be covered with a tarp branches and leaves.

3. Three-Sided Lean-To or Debris Hut:

- Construct a framework similar to a den, using branches.
- Then use leaves, grass, or other organic materials to insulate the interior of the structure after piling them on top.

- Fire Pit: Establish a designated fire pit at a distance from your shelter that is sufficient for safety. Construct a ring around the fire using rocks, and make sure you have plenty of wood nearby to keep the fire going.
- Collecting Water: If you have access to large enough leaves, a tarp, or a container, you should try to construct a rainwater collection system. This will ensure that there is a supply of pure water.

- First Aid Station: Arrange all of your first aid items inside of a bag or container that is watertight, and then put it in a location within your basecamp that is easily accessible.

4.3. SAFETY & STRENGTH OF SHELTER

It is essential to your ability to survive in the wilderness that you take precautions to ensure the stability and security of your shelter:

- Protection from Weather: On the roof and the walls of your shelter, construct an additional layer that is thick and insulating by using additional materials such as leaves, moss, or pine boughs. This helps you stay warm and prevents you from getting wet.
- Firmness: Be sure that all of the logs and branches that you are using to create the shelter are firmly attached to one another so that it does not fall apart in the event of heavy rain or wind.
- Fire Hazard Safety: Fire safety requires that you retain command of the blaze at all times and keep the fire pit at a respectable distance from your shelter. To reduce the risk of fires starting by mistake, sweep away any dead leaves or debris that may be in the vicinity.

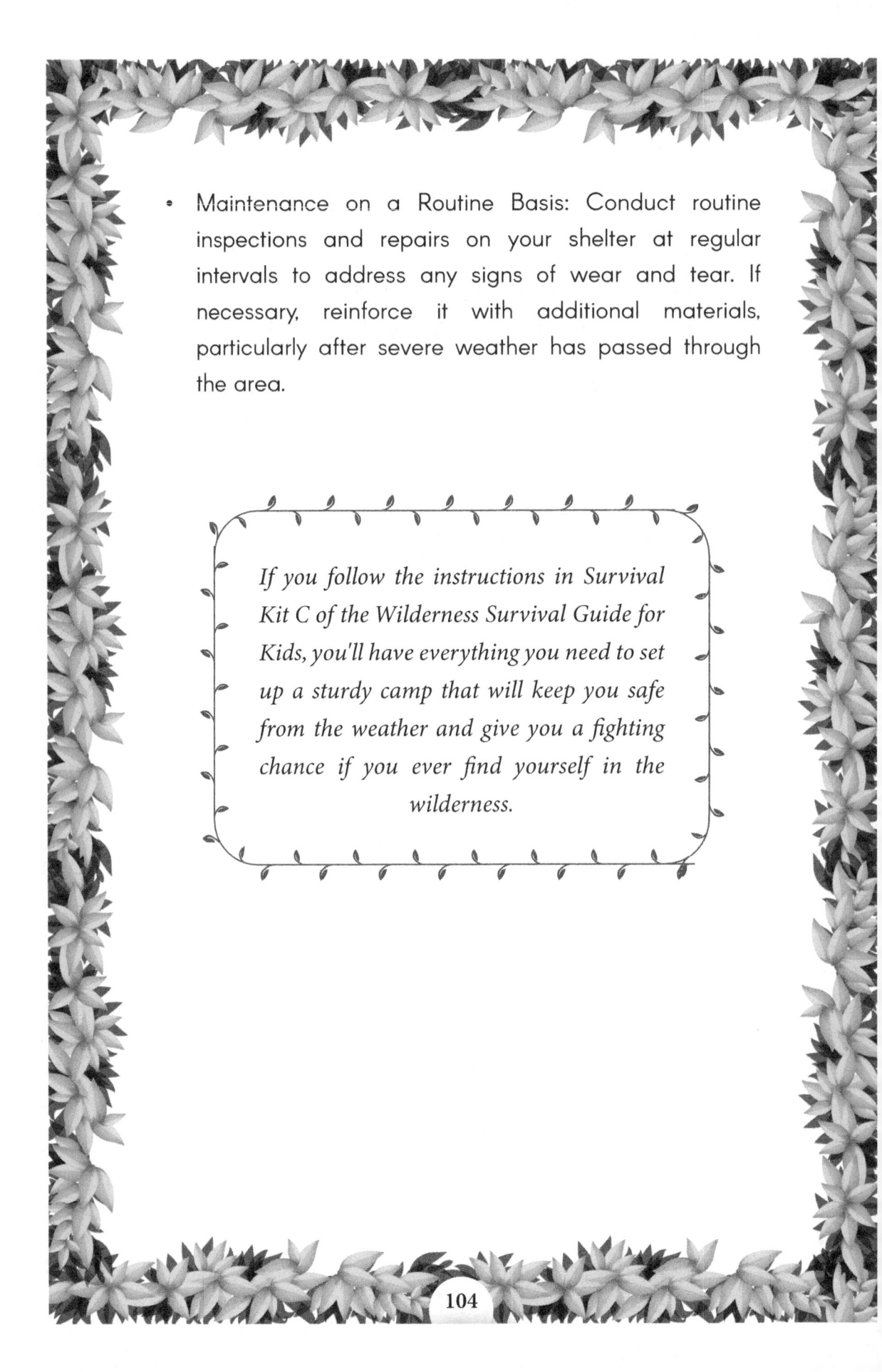

- Maintenance on a Routine Basis: Conduct routine inspections and repairs on your shelter at regular intervals to address any signs of wear and tear. If necessary, reinforce it with additional materials, particularly after severe weather has passed through the area.

> *If you follow the instructions in Survival Kit C of the Wilderness Survival Guide for Kids, you'll have everything you need to set up a sturdy camp that will keep you safe from the weather and give you a fighting chance if you ever find yourself in the wilderness.*

PART 5
VITALITY SKILLS

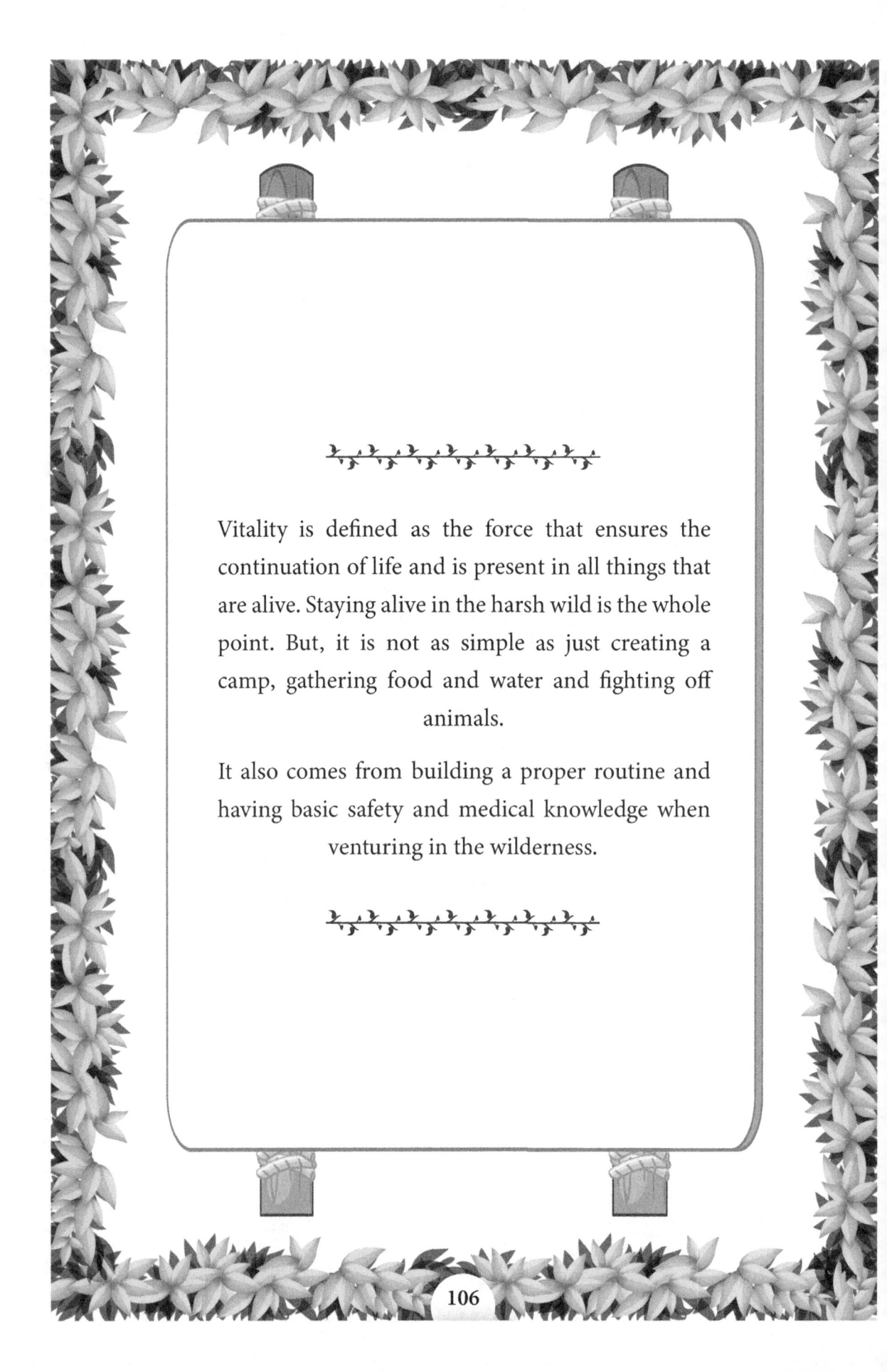

Vitality is defined as the force that ensures the continuation of life and is present in all things that are alive. Staying alive in the harsh wild is the whole point. But, it is not as simple as just creating a camp, gathering food and water and fighting off animals.

It also comes from building a proper routine and having basic safety and medical knowledge when venturing in the wilderness.

SURVIVAL KIT D STAYING ALIVE/SURVIVING

The next matter of survival is well…survival. I mean, literally stay alive is what this book is all about, surely from the previous sections we have seen survival strategies. But this chapter deals with how to stay alive and keep your health in check.

5.1. FIRST AID

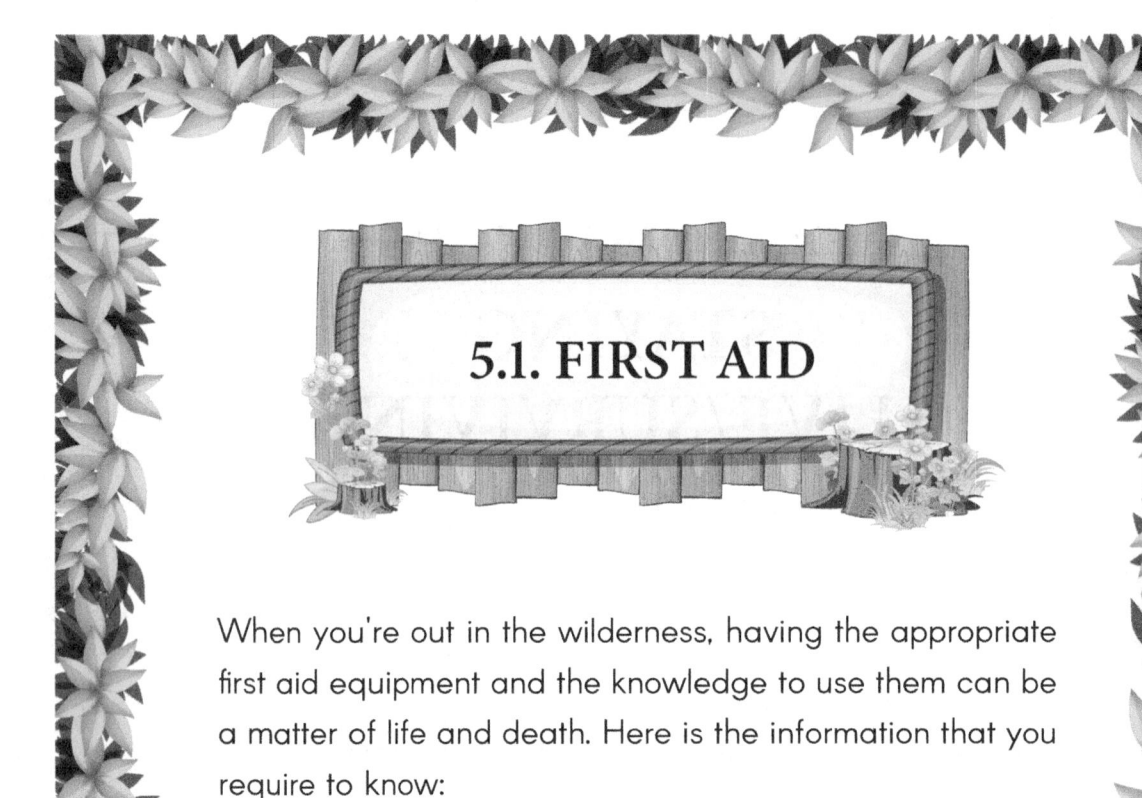

When you're out in the wilderness, having the appropriate first aid equipment and the knowledge to use them can be a matter of life and death. Here is the information that you require to know:

Essentials for a First Aid Kit

Your wilderness first aid kit should include the following essentials: adhesive bandages, gauze, antiseptic wipes, tweezers, scissors, adhesive tape, pain killers, allergy medication (if necessary), and any other personal medications or medical supplies. A guide on providing first aid is also very helpful.

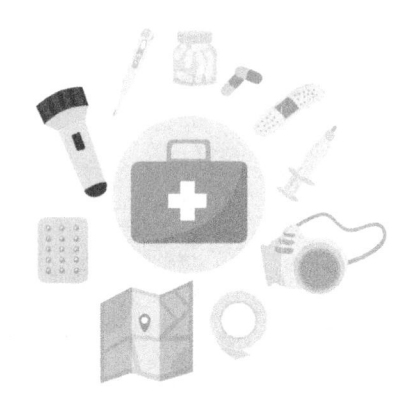

How to Care for a Minor Cut or Scrape

- Size and Depth of the Wound: By carefully examining the wound, you can assess both its size and its depth. Examine the patient for any symptoms of infection.
- Disinfection: The wound should be cleaned using antiseptic wipes, and the region around the wound should also be cleaned.
- Adhesive Bandage: To prevent infection, cover any small wounds or abrasions with an adhesive bandage and apply pressure to the area.
- Dress a Larger Wound: To cover and protect an area that has a larger wound, use sterile gauze and adhesive tape.
- Stop the Bleeding: To stop the bleeding, apply light pressure with a clean cloth or gauze and secure it with sterile tape.
- Decontamination: Raise the injured area above ground level, it at all possible. To minimize chances of contamination from dirt.

5.2. BUILDING A FIRE

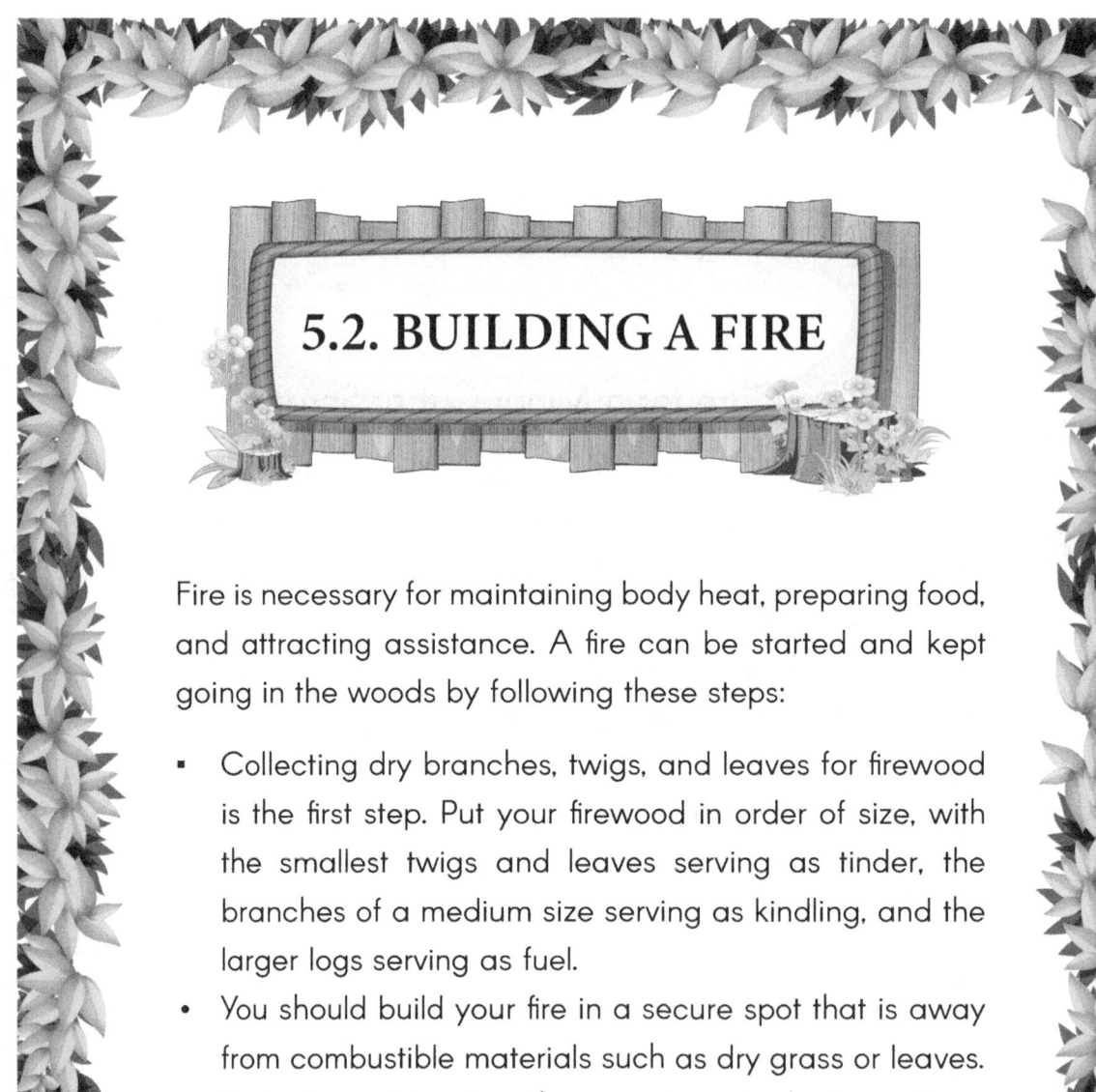

Fire is necessary for maintaining body heat, preparing food, and attracting assistance. A fire can be started and kept going in the woods by following these steps:

- Collecting dry branches, twigs, and leaves for firewood is the first step. Put your firewood in order of size, with the smallest twigs and leaves serving as tinder, the branches of a medium size serving as kindling, and the larger logs serving as fuel.
- You should build your fire in a secure spot that is away from combustible materials such as dry grass or leaves. If at all possible, clear the area down to the bare dirt.
- Using your kindling, build a structure in the shape of a teepee or a log home. Put the tinder in the middle of the fire.
- To ignite the tinder, you can either use a fire starter or matches. Just a light breeze will do to fan the flames.
- To keep the fire burning, gradually add additional kindling and eventually fuel logs to the fire while maintaining a proper balance.

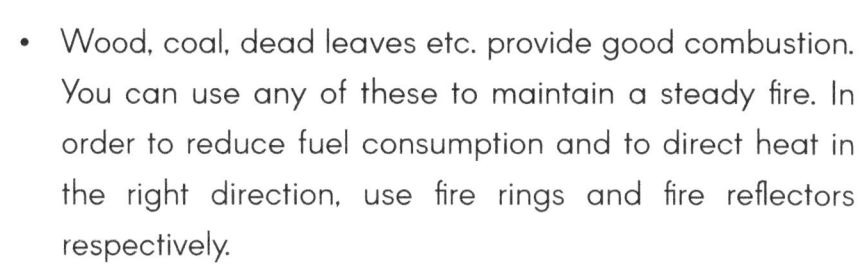

- Wood, coal, dead leaves etc. provide good combustion. You can use any of these to maintain a steady fire. In order to reduce fuel consumption and to direct heat in the right direction, use fire rings and fire reflectors respectively.
- Always make sure not to leave any evidence of your fire behind. When you are about to leave, you must put out the fire using water and camouflage the ashes in the dirt by string them.

5.3. TRACKING & NAVIGATION

It is absolutely necessary for you to maintain your orientation and locate your basecamp in order to survive. What you ought to do is as follows:

- Before you head out, make sure to make a mental image of the important landmarks, directions and position of the sun in that area. Familiarize yourself with the map and assess the environment around you.
- Leave trail markers along the way using things like ribbons, stones, carvings on tree barks etc. This will help you to find your way back much easier as you traverse the area.
- Reference points must always be noted. Unique characteristics of natural things such as tress, lakes and landscapes can be mapped in your head as a visual cue to help in better navigation.
- Always have a compass on you, and make sure you know how to use it. A GPS device can also be useful.

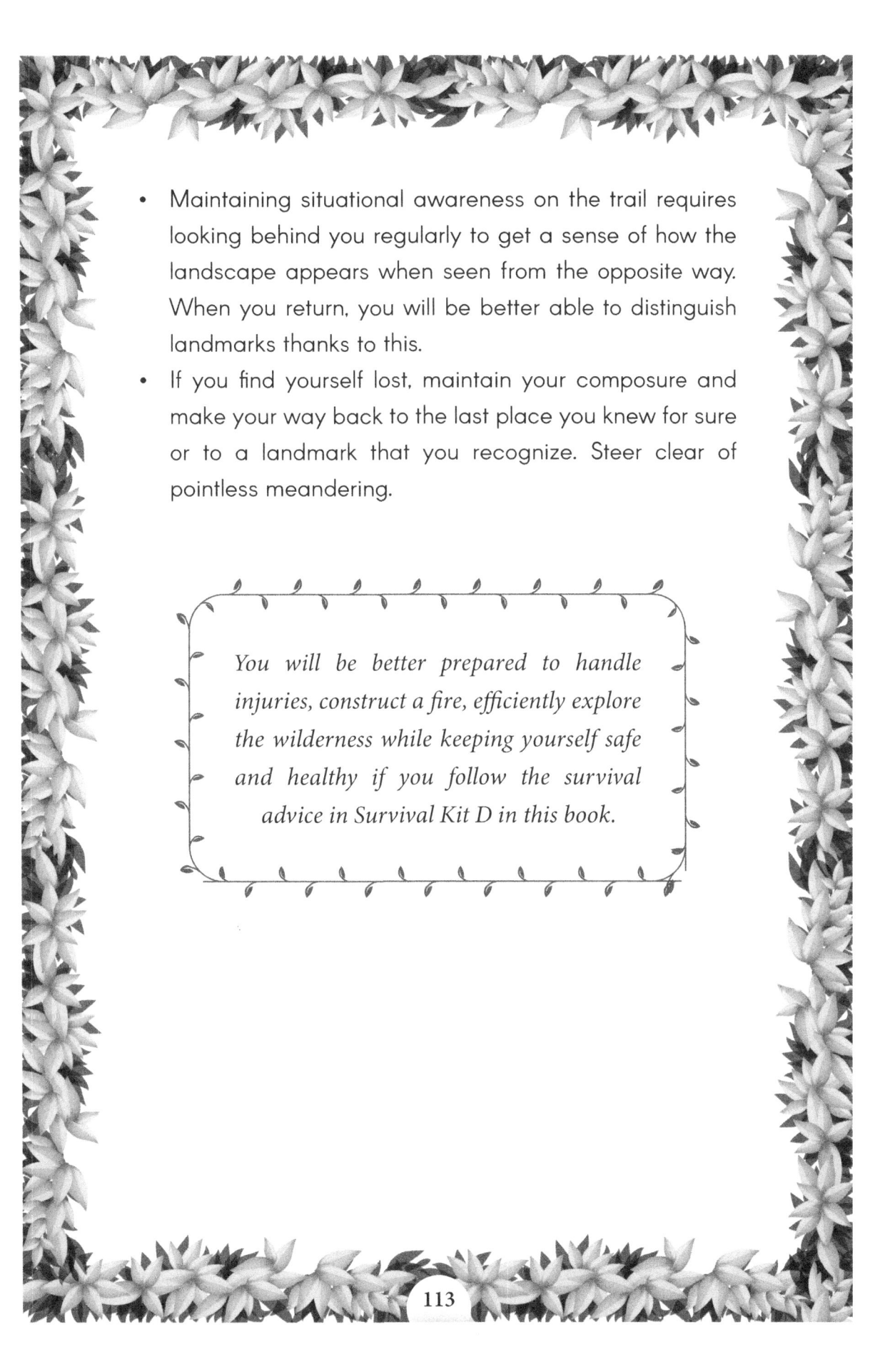

- Maintaining situational awareness on the trail requires looking behind you regularly to get a sense of how the landscape appears when seen from the opposite way. When you return, you will be better able to distinguish landmarks thanks to this.
- If you find yourself lost, maintain your composure and make your way back to the last place you knew for sure or to a landmark that you recognize. Steer clear of pointless meandering.

> *You will be better prepared to handle injuries, construct a fire, efficiently explore the wilderness while keeping yourself safe and healthy if you follow the survival advice in Survival Kit D in this book.*

PART 6
THE CAMPY KID

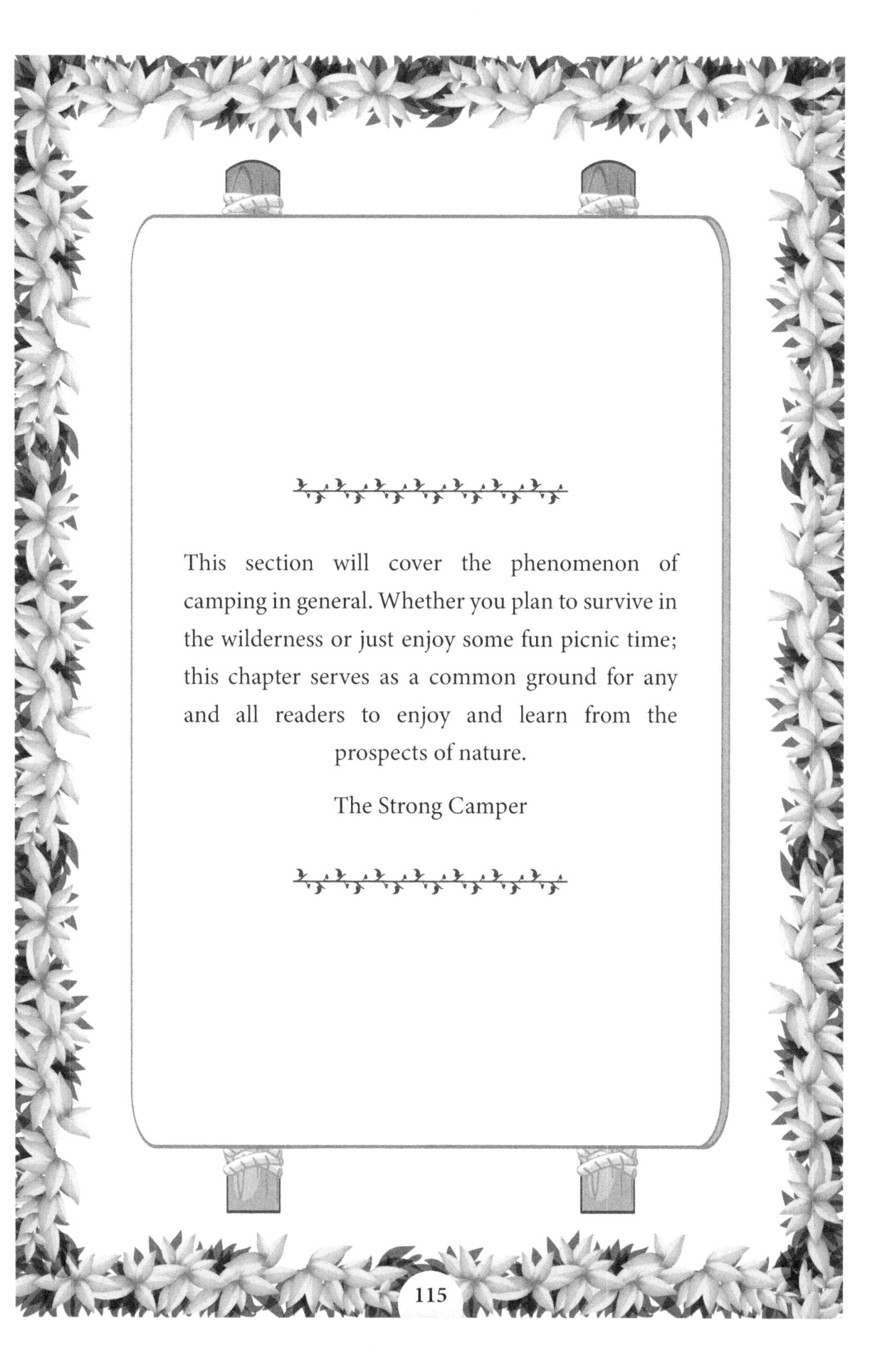

This section will cover the phenomenon of camping in general. Whether you plan to survive in the wilderness or just enjoy some fun picnic time; this chapter serves as a common ground for any and all readers to enjoy and learn from the prospects of nature.

The Strong Camper

6.1. PLANNING

Please look at the "How I Plan To Survive" worksheet.

How I Plan To Survive

Now that you know many things related to wilderness from the previous chapters. Write down an extensive survival plan by highlighting your goals. These goals should be exclusive. I suggest making a diagrammatic representation by making a flowchart.

6.2. HOW TO READ MAPS

Being in the outdoors and having to fend for oneself can be a thrilling adventure, but it can also be difficult. The ability to read maps is an important skill that will not only help you explore the great outdoors, but will also assist keep you safe. This is an easy-to-follow tutorial for children that will teach them how to read maps so that they can survive in the wilderness.

Begin with gaining a grasp of the fundamental components of a map. Carefully read the "Cartographer Kid" manual.

Cartographer Kid

Symbols

Discover the meanings behind the many symbols that are used to symbolize things like mountains, rivers, and highways.

Scale

Accurate measurement of distances requires an understanding of the scale used.

Compass Rose

Use the compass rose to determine which direction on the map is north, south, east, and west.

Orient Yourself

Find your bearings by locating the north on a map with a compass or by using natural landmarks. When you have determined the location of north, you may then arrange the map in the appropriate manner.

Keep to the Contour Lines

Contour lines on a map depict the change in elevation from one point to the next. When lines are close together, the terrain is steep, and when lines are far apart, the ground is gentle.

Calculate the Required Distance

Make use of the scale on the map to determine how far you will need to travel. It's possible that one inch on the map corresponds to one mile, for instance.

Prepare Your Itinerary

Determine both where you currently are and where you intend to go, as well as any potential obstacles, such as cliffs or wetlands. Create a route that is both secure and time-effective.

Stay on Track

While you are traveling, make sure to check the map at regular intervals to confirm that you are traveling along the route that you had planned. Look around for recognizable landmarks to help you pinpoint your position.

Adjust for the Terrain

It is important to have an understanding of how the various terrains effect your journey. Take it easy on the steep inclines, and map out your river crossings ahead of time.

Have patience, learning to read a map takes practice. Do not allow yourself to become disheartened when you make errors; learning is an essential aspect of experiencing new things.

6.3. EXPLORING THE WILDERNESS

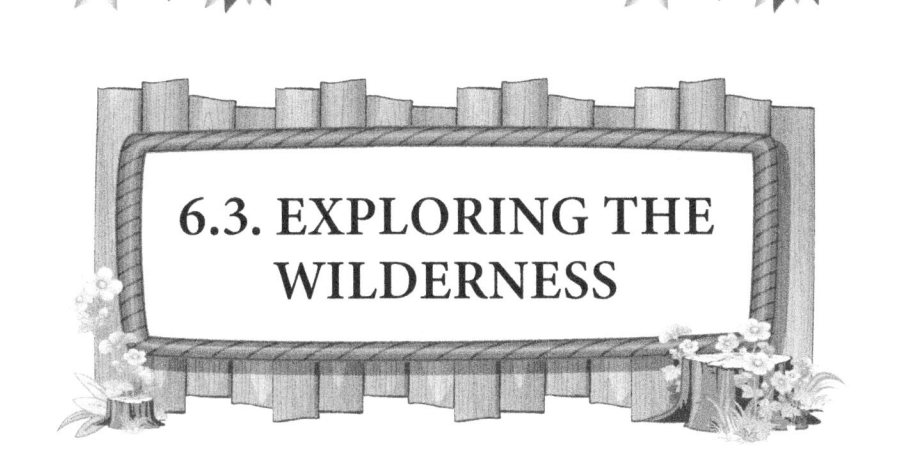

Please look at the "Nature's Checklist" worksheet.

In this tabulated checklist, please record your daily findings from the wilderness and record how you have used these items.

Days	Findings	Quantity Acquired	Quantity Used	Quantity Discarded

6.4. WHAT ARE YOU PACKING?

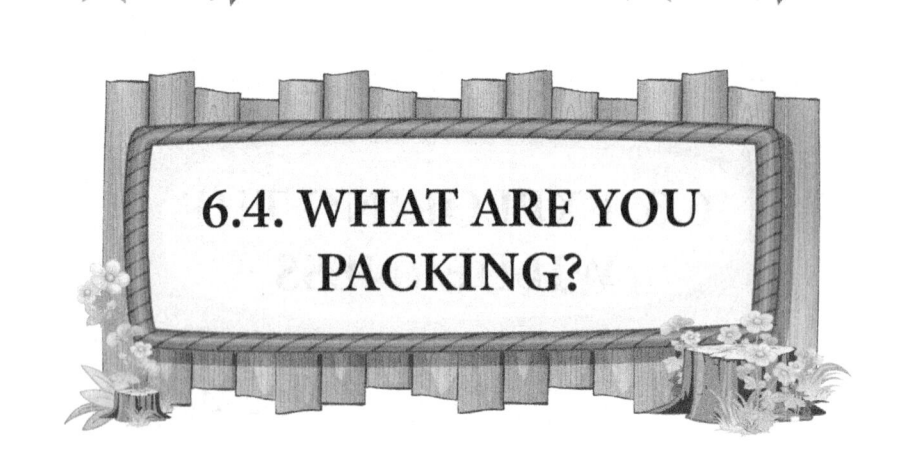

Please look at the "Wilderness Satchel" worksheet.

In this worksheet, make a list of what things do you consider to be ideal for a wilderness exploring journey. With each thing, write down how this will help you in your adventure.

Wilderness Satchel

Enlist the things you will add to your backpack, in the answer lines, write its quantity and reason why you think is important to add.

1. _____

_____

2. _____

_____

3. _____

_____

4. _____

_____

5. _____

_____

6. _____

_____

7. _____

_____

8. _____

_____

9. _____

_____

10. _____

_____

6.5. OUTDOOR COOKING

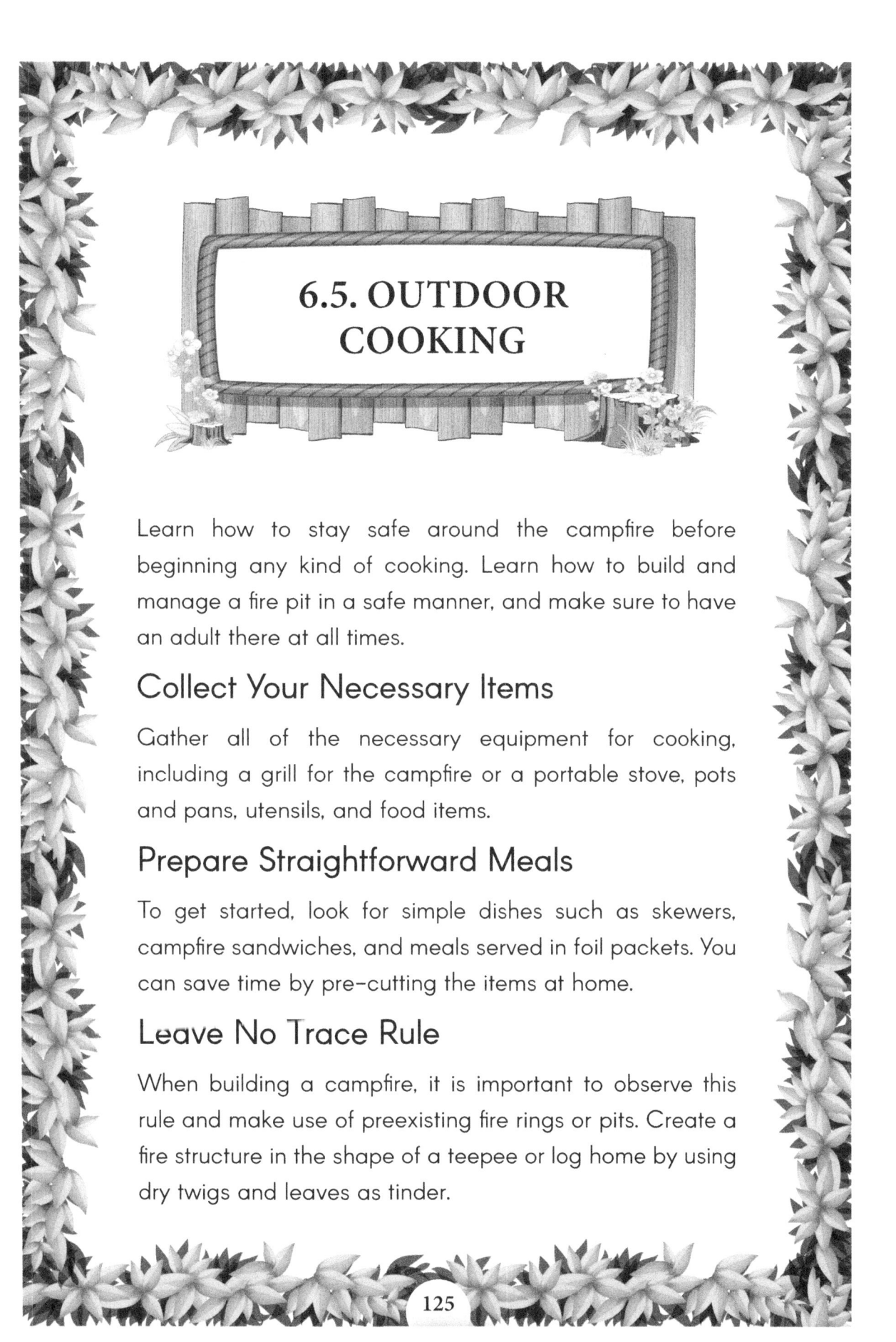

Learn how to stay safe around the campfire before beginning any kind of cooking. Learn how to build and manage a fire pit in a safe manner, and make sure to have an adult there at all times.

Collect Your Necessary Items

Gather all of the necessary equipment for cooking, including a grill for the campfire or a portable stove, pots and pans, utensils, and food items.

Prepare Straightforward Meals

To get started, look for simple dishes such as skewers, campfire sandwiches, and meals served in foil packets. You can save time by pre-cutting the items at home.

Leave No Trace Rule

When building a campfire, it is important to observe this rule and make use of preexisting fire rings or pits. Create a fire structure in the shape of a teepee or log home by using dry twigs and leaves as tinder.

Managing Your Fire

Learn how to regulate the fire's intensity as well as its size to ensure your safety. In order to put out the fire, you need to put on protective gloves and keep a bucket of water or sand nearby.

Clean as You Go

Maintain the cleanliness of the campsite by cleaning the dishes as soon as they are used. Use soap that breaks down naturally, and adhere to the "Leave No Trace" standards.

Etiquette for the Wilderness

Show respect for nature by not over picking flora and avoiding upsetting wildlife. Food scraps should be disposed of in the right manner.

Sweet Wilderness

Campfire desserts like s'mores, campfire banana boats, and roasted marshmallows are always a crowd pleaser and shouldn't be forgotten.

Memories

The act of preparing food outside in the fresh air is an excellent method to strengthen relationships with one's family and friends. Create some unforgettable dinners together while you show off your abilities in the great outdoors.

6.6. UPWARD LEAP

Proper technique, safety measures, and reverence for the tree are all essential for tree climbing success. Here is a basic overview of tree climbing:

First, Select An Appropriate Tree

- Choose a tree with a clear trunk structure and strong, durable limbs. Low-hanging branches are preferable.
- Look for rot, sickness, or injury to determine the tree's overall health.

Second, Evaluate Dangers & Safety

- Be aware of possible harmful things around you such as thorns, dangling branches, bug nests, quicksand, geysers etc.
- Make sure there's enough room to climb the tree without getting stuck.
- Think about the weather, and don't go climbing if there's a chance of a storm, snow, or ice.

Third, Use Proper Attributes & Clothing

You should be able to move around with ease and freedom, so be sure to wear clothes that fit will but are also loose or elastic to allow proper flexibility.

- Detach any hanging accessories or tags etc. from the clothes.
- It is best to wear long sleeves and full length pants to allow minimum direct exposure of your skin.
- Non-slip shoes with a firm grip and excellent durability are recommended for climbing purposes. You can also climb barefooted.
- Assess the height and dimensions of the object you wish to climb and accordingly use, climbing ropes, harness and a helmet.
- For further advice on climbing and related knowledge, you must consult seasoned mountaineers.

Fourth, Get Your Muscles Ready

Stretching your arms, back and legs a little before any physical activity allows for more flexibility and reduces the chances of strains on your muscles.

Fifth, Test Of Branch Strength

- Prior to putting your weight on the branch, test its agility by putting a firm amount of force on it.
- Begin by giving the branch a light shake or a good bounce.

- If your assessment points to the tree being climbable Then start your upward leap.
- Weak, thin, or fragile branches must be avoided.

Sixth, The Safety Tip

- "Use Three Points Of Contact," is a safety protocol for climbing trees. It means to always keep three contact points in mind during your climb.
- This involves grasping the tree or its branches with either one foot and two hands, or vice versa.
- Better stability and a stronger grip is attained through this safety method.

Seventh, Plan Your Climb

- Formulate your climbing pattern and direction after assessing which portions are good for footholds and for hand grabs.
- Try to find logical inflection points or branching patterns.
- Take it easy, climb gently, and check your footing before you make any moves.

Eighth, Be Aware Of Your Surroundings

- Watch out for potential dangers while you climb.
- Keep an eye out for other climbers, tense branches, and other potential impediments.
- Do not destroy the tree or disturb any nesting birds.

Ninth, Descend Safely

- Take your time and be cautious as you make your way down; this is safety rule number nine.
- When climbing, go backwards to check the stability of each branch and foothold before using them.
- Instead of jumping or freefalling from the tree, try moving carefully.

Tenth, Treat The Tree And Its Surroundings With The Utmost Reverence

- Do not bend or break branches too much, and don't hurt the tree or the plants around it.
- Don't forget to pack up your trash and stuff before you depart.

6.7. FISHFUL THINKING

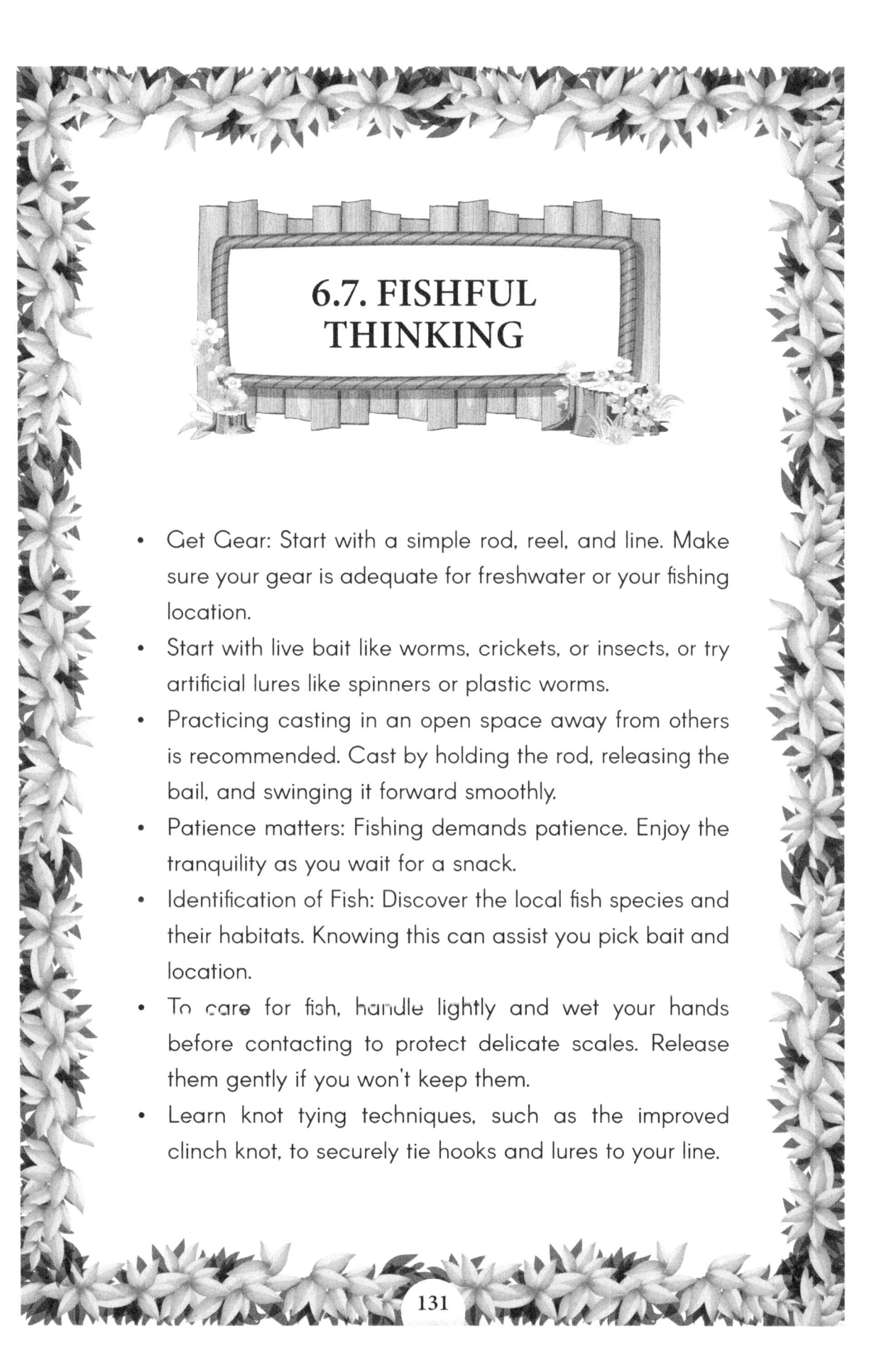

- Get Gear: Start with a simple rod, reel, and line. Make sure your gear is adequate for freshwater or your fishing location.
- Start with live bait like worms, crickets, or insects, or try artificial lures like spinners or plastic worms.
- Practicing casting in an open space away from others is recommended. Cast by holding the rod, releasing the bail, and swinging it forward smoothly.
- Patience matters: Fishing demands patience. Enjoy the tranquility as you wait for a snack.
- Identification of Fish: Discover the local fish species and their habitats. Knowing this can assist you pick bait and location.
- To care for fish, handle lightly and wet your hands before contacting to protect delicate scales. Release them gently if you won't keep them.
- Learn knot tying techniques, such as the improved clinch knot, to securely tie hooks and lures to your line.

- Be aware of local fishing regulations, such as catch limits, size limitations, and license requirements.
- For safety, always use a life jacket when fishing from a boat or near deep water. Be alert of hooks and your surroundings.
- Leave No Trace: Properly dispose of fishing lines, hooks, and rubbish to safeguard the environment and wildlife.

6.8. MUST WRITE!

Look at the "My Survival Log" worksheet.

In this worksheet, be free to write anything, from past wilderness experiences to potential future wilderness plans. You can write all the recent information, tips and tricks you learned from outside this book.

Think of this as a record sheet for use in wilderness.

My Survival Log

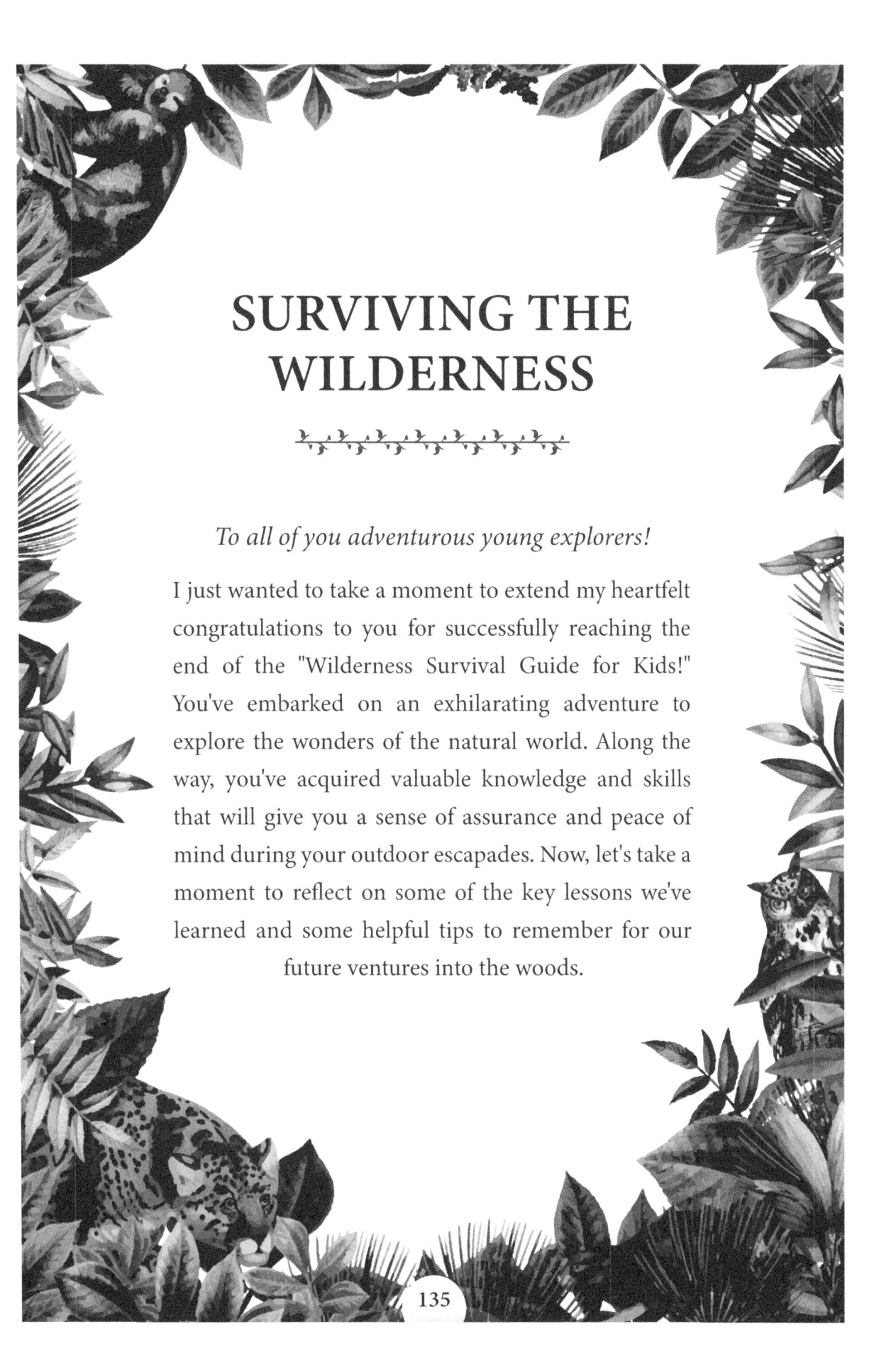

SURVIVING THE WILDERNESS

To all of you adventurous young explorers!

I just wanted to take a moment to extend my heartfelt congratulations to you for successfully reaching the end of the "Wilderness Survival Guide for Kids!" You've embarked on an exhilarating adventure to explore the wonders of the natural world. Along the way, you've acquired valuable knowledge and skills that will give you a sense of assurance and peace of mind during your outdoor escapades. Now, let's take a moment to reflect on some of the key lessons we've learned and some helpful tips to remember for our future ventures into the woods.

Let's Retrack Some Important Ideas

Be The Cool Kid: You now have the knowledge and skills necessary to overcome any difficulty in nature. So, stay calm and think carefully at each step.

Personal Security: In other words; your safety. This should your first and foremost step. Always keep others informed your plans and double check your things and facts before venturing out into the wild.

Constructing a Shelter: The structures, called shelters that will safeguard you from the dangerous weather and effects of the wilderness, you have learned how to make them as per your situation and requirements.

Starting A Fire: Think of fire as your closest companion when you are out in the wilderness. You have learned how to light a fire using a variety of techniques, such as a magnifying glass or a fire starter. Exercise these skills, but always keep safety in mind when working with fire.

Water Management: To ensure one's continued existence, one must have access to clean water. You are now familiar with the techniques necessary to gather and filter water from natural sources. Always make maintaining proper hydration a top priority.

Foraging for Food: You've gained the ability to recognize secure choices through the process of foraging for edible plants. However, you should never consume any plant until you are 100 percent positive that it is safe to do so. If at all possible, steer clear of it.

Health n Medical: Your knowledge of first aid can make the difference between life and death. It is important to keep in mind how to treat common injuries such as cuts, sprains, and insect bites, as well as the ABCs, which stand for airway, breathing, and circulation.

Navigation Expert: You have honed your ability to navigate unfamiliar terrain by familiarizing yourself with a variety of maps and compasses through various outdoor activities. Maintain these tools in your possession at all times and be familiar with their use.

Your Checklist for the Fight for Survival

It is critical to run through a checklist in order to ensure that you are well-equipped for each outing in the outdoors that you undertake, including the following items:

- Be sure to dress appropriately for the conditions by donning layers. Keep in mind to bring shoes that comfortable yet sturdy.
- Always check your bag thoroughly before and after leaving for your adventure Make sure it has these things; first-aid box, flashlight, ration bars etc.
- Always carry either a map or a GPS device with you at all times. A compass is also good, but you should know how to use all these things.
- A not-so-heavy tarp or an emergency blanket should be kept in case building a shelter. This will be an essential component.
- Containers to store water, such as bottles and things that can purify water must also be carried.
- You must always be prepared for any emergency contact with a fully charged backup cellphone, a whistle or a signal mirror.

Let's Retrack Some Important Ideas

Keep in mind that each and every experience you have in the wild is an opportunity for you to learn and develop. The following are some parting words of advice that you should keep in mind:

- Safe exploration is the name of the game when it comes to the adventure genre, but you should never put your safety at risk. Always make sure someone is aware of your plans and the time you anticipate returning.
- Treat the wilderness with care and respect, as nature deserves to be treated. Leave no sign of your presence and stay away from the local flora and fauna at all costs.
- Always Be Willing to Learn: Acquiring the Knowledge and Skills Necessary to Survive is a Lifelong Process. If you continue to educate yourself and hone your skills, you will eventually become a wild game expert.
- You may experience the beauty of nature together while also sharing your knowledge and experiences with your loved ones and friends.
- The wild has many secrets that are just waiting to be discovered. Be open of heart and mind and your sense of wonder will take you.

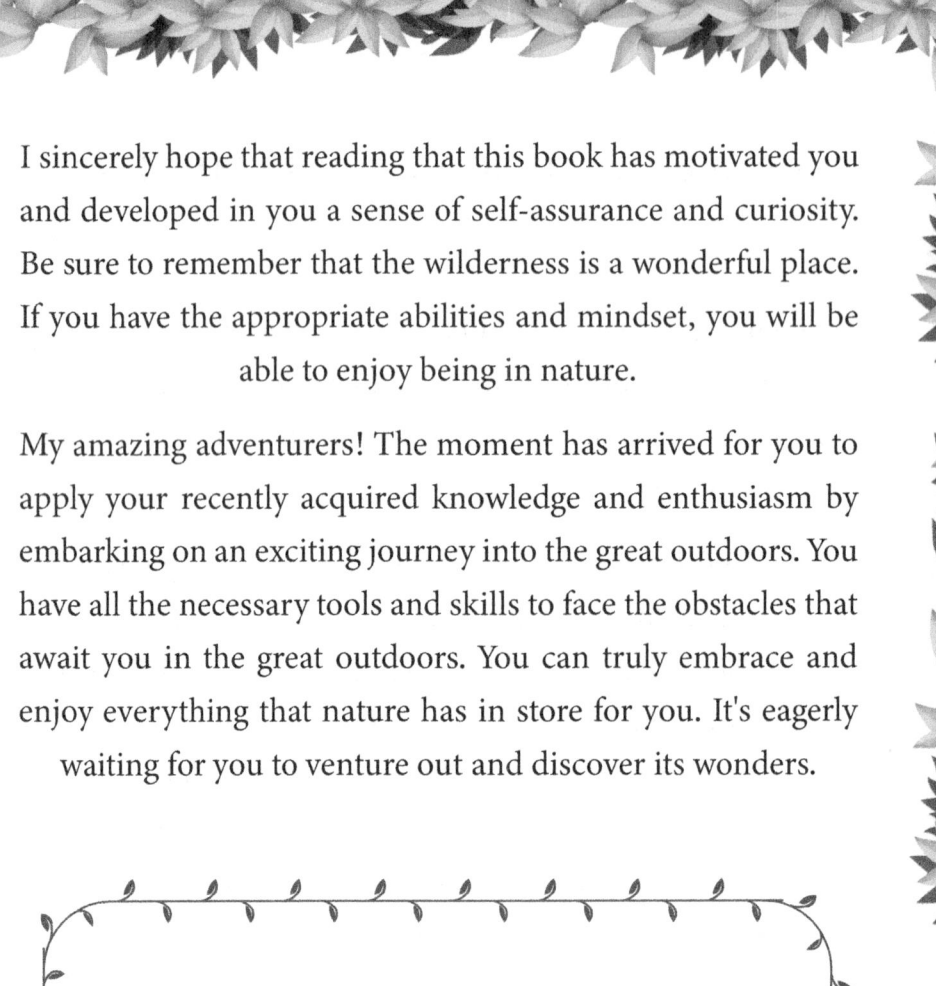

I sincerely hope that reading that this book has motivated you and developed in you a sense of self-assurance and curiosity. Be sure to remember that the wilderness is a wonderful place. If you have the appropriate abilities and mindset, you will be able to enjoy being in nature.

My amazing adventurers! The moment has arrived for you to apply your recently acquired knowledge and enthusiasm by embarking on an exciting journey into the great outdoors. You have all the necessary tools and skills to face the obstacles that await you in the great outdoors. You can truly embrace and enjoy everything that nature has in store for you. It's eagerly waiting for you to venture out and discover its wonders.

It's important to exercise caution, but at the same time, it's crucial to maintain a sense of adventure and keep the spirit of discovery alive in your hearts.

Wish you all the best for your adventures!

With best regards

Your Guides on Defending Yourself in the Wild

ABOUT THE AUTHOR

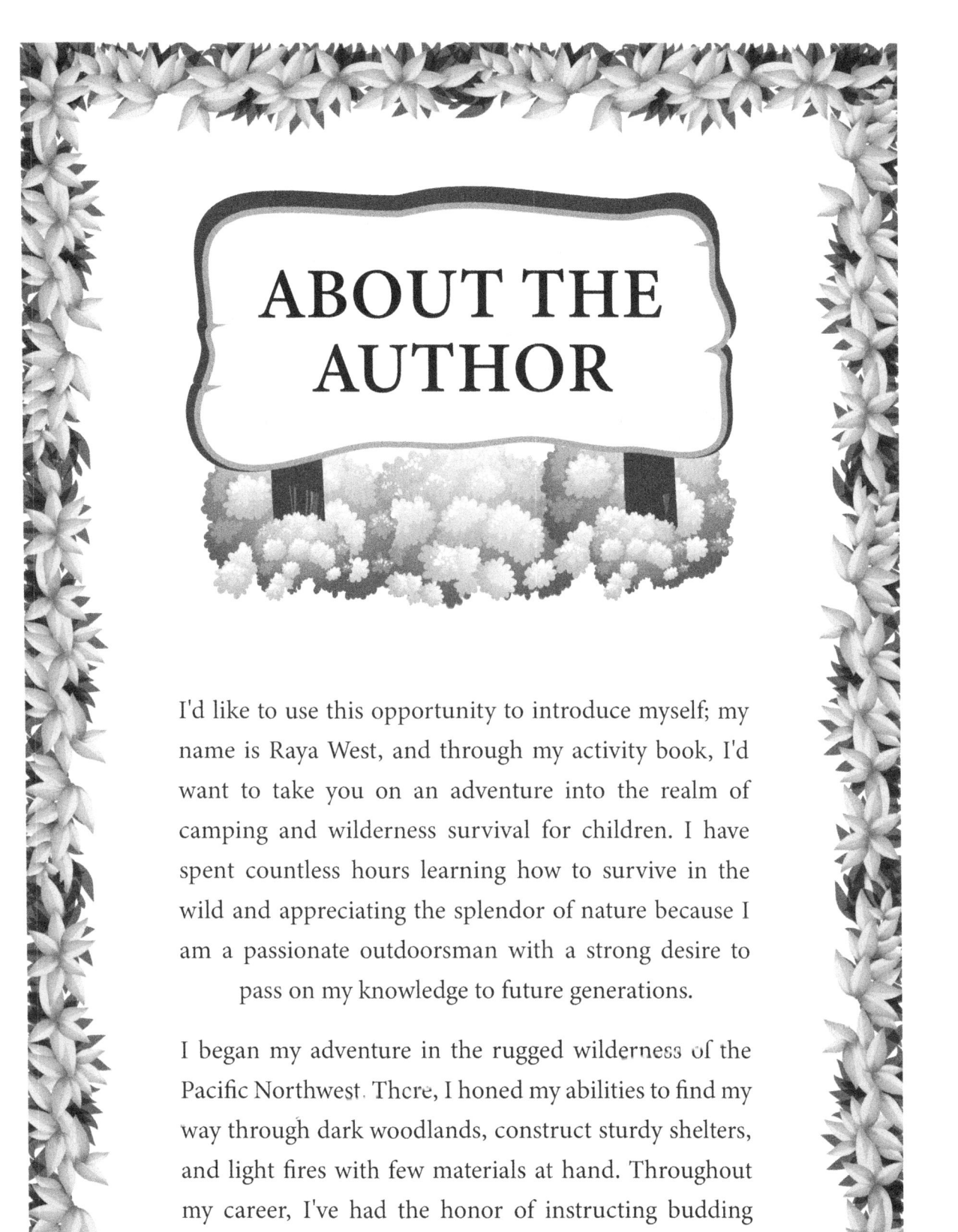

I'd like to use this opportunity to introduce myself; my name is Raya West, and through my activity book, I'd want to take you on an adventure into the realm of camping and wilderness survival for children. I have spent countless hours learning how to survive in the wild and appreciating the splendor of nature because I am a passionate outdoorsman with a strong desire to pass on my knowledge to future generations.

I began my adventure in the rugged wilderness of the Pacific Northwest. There, I honed my abilities to find my way through dark woodlands, construct sturdy shelters, and light fires with few materials at hand. Throughout my career, I've had the honor of instructing budding explorers in these techniques, sparking their interest in the outdoors and inspiring them to treat it with the respect it deserves.

My goal in writing this book is to help young readers develop a strong feeling of self-reliance, confidence, and appreciation for the natural world. It's more than just figuring out how to stay alive. A love of nature and an appreciation for the lessons it may teach us are equally crucial.

I take groups of young explorers on camping vacations full of fun and exciting new experiences. Everything from pitching a tent in the open air to foraging for food in the woods falls under this category. We will discover the hidden wonders of nature and create memories that will last a lifetime.

Help me encourage the next generation to appreciate the wonders of the outdoors by joining me on this exciting journey to teach them valuable skills and instill in them a love for the natural world. Do you want to join me on this exciting adventure?

Made in the USA
Las Vegas, NV
11 February 2024